To my dad,
David Marshall Gessner

## A Pocket of Grace

An unexplainable blessing or circumstance in which God directs your path in ways you never dreamed or imagined.

# TABLE OF CONTENTS

# ACKNOWLEDGEMENTS

I am deeply grateful for the encouragement and guidance of my colleagues, friends, and family.

Tom Bird, my editor, who pushed me just enough, never gave up on me, and believes in my Divine Author Within.

Jonathan Auman, my stepson, who graciously helped me with formatting.

Jennifer Flynn, my business coach, who held a BIG vision for me while I was writing and guided me in using the book to serve others through my coaching practice.

Hadley Kifner, my colleague and good friend who heard about the heron, baby feathers, and Saints Hildegard, Julian, and Brigid, for many years when we worked as chaplains together. Thank you for repeatedly insisting I could write this book, your editorial skills, and your memory.

Debby Mead, my best friend, whose voice was often my conscience, whispering (at times loudly) what I needed to hear, even when it was hard.

David Gessner, my older brother, whose writing skills and feedback, fine tuning of family details, and cheering, buoyed me forward.

For the saints, living and dead, whose wisdom guided me and informs me still. Too many to name, hopefully you know who you are.

For former patients, families, group members, students, and others I've had the honor of companioning with. Thank you for trusting me and for sharing your stories.

For my children, Noah and Addie; and my stepson Micah, who love and root for me always.

For Tim, my beloved, who loves me, offered helpful insights and reflective questions, brought me coffee, and always has my back.

For God, the One who found me at my lowest point and has stuck around ever since.

# INTRODUCTION

"Instructions for life:
Pay attention. Be amazed. Tell about it."
~Mary Oliver

In some ways, I'm re-mothering myself with this book. In the process of writing, a love song to my own heart emerged. Unexpected healing arrived while I was writing, and my hope is that it will be a love song to your heart as well.

I'm writing these pages as we re-emerge from the global "coronavirus (COVID-19)" health pandemic. I've wanted to write this book for years, but now seems to be the right time, because everyone on the planet is collectively grieving. People feel more alone and frightened than ever. Many are dying, or sick, and their loved ones are mourning, starving for connection, and hungry for spiritual sustenance.

Grief also happens to be my area of expertise, although as my grief counselor and friend Jane says, you're always learning, and surprised at how much you don't know. For nearly 20 years, I worked as a palliative-care and bereavement chaplain, an end-of-life specialist of sorts, in a level one trauma center. In doing so, I witnessed hundreds of deaths, from a newborn with failure to thrive, clinging to life; a 25-year-old opera singer with a rare heart disorder; to a 43-year-old mother of four who died in a car crash; and an 88-year-old with terminal cancer who was at peace with dying.

The similarities among people at the end of their lives are uncanny. We want a sense of completion, to know that our lives have meaning. We want to retain a sense of dignity. And we want to leave a legacy for those we love; a piece of us that will live on, for the greater good.

In my work, I support people who experience loss and help them connect with the transformative power of grief, so that they can live purpose-fully and joy-fully. My family-practice physician told me once that approximately five family members are affected by the death of a loved one. Facilitating healthy grieving is one way to help people integrate their grief more proactively. I've accompanied countless men and women who've moved through and integrated their loss into the fabric of their lives.

I've mentored many chaplain students as well, and see my primary role as a spiritual companion, fostering spiritual awareness. As spiritual teacher and author Eckhart Tolle says, "Awareness is the greatest agent of change." Over and over, while journeying with individuals, I come back to the core message I learned during my first major loss.

My world was turned upside down when my beloved, yet complicated, father was diagnosed with terminal lung cancer during my heartbreaking divorce. Struggling with despair about life and my purpose, I received an unexpected visit from a mysterious, benevolent guest with the important message: *You are not alone!*

These comforting words were followed by serendipitist events and synchronicities. I was captured in some magical stream that flowed simultaneously alongside my father's dying and my marriage's death. Side by side was the unimaginable reality of terminal illness — the end looming, *and* the ethereal aspect — I was held and being carried through, step by step.

At the threshold of death, I found connection, meaning, and depth. Following the nudges led me on an unexpected path of discovery and to my vocation as a hospital chaplain.

*You are not alone* became the foundation of my life and later the cornerstone of my chaplaincy. My moment of wonderment planted a seed, invited me to work with dying and bereaved people so they wouldn't feel alone, either. The deeper calling though, is to help others — *you* perhaps— tap into the sacred flow of life.

While I was going through this most difficult time in my life, I experienced deep healing as well. I witnessed my father's humor, fear, and most authentic self as he fought for his life. In many ways, grief woke me up. It was a nascent time when I discovered a deeper side of myself — a dormant, yet starving, suffering, spiritual side.

This wasn't the first time I craved something deeper. When I was 17 years old, I recall standing in the circular driveway of our home after playing tennis. I pondered, *There must be more than this.*

At the heart of my vision is an experience of the divine — the deeply personal nature of the Universe and my transformation from the grace I received. There are different paths to awakened consciousness — mine was through grief and grace.

It is said there is often a hidden treasure buried in crisis, that there's always a positive element within it. Often crisis is the vehicle, and it opens us up enough to accept a different perspective, and more readily surrender to the flow of life. This was certainly true for me.

In addition to collectively grieving, we live in a time of collective awakening as well. Because of the global pandemic, many people express not wanting to go back to the way things were and are hoping for a new way forward — something deeper and of more value. We've learned what matters most during this time and are asking the questions: How does my life have value? How shall I move forward? What is on the other side?

In this unprecedented time there is an urgent need for us all to step up. We can't afford to play small. The world needs us to elevate ourselves, cultivate our gifts and to share them— for each other, our children, grandchildren, and the future of our planet.

Perhaps you're grieving a loved one, or dealing with an illness, are a family caregiver, or just worn out, tired of all the societal and political upheaval. Maybe you're hoping to be pulled forward into something new.

This book points one way forward. In the pages that follow, I will share what I've experienced and seen repeatedly in my work with dying and bereaved people. Many of the ways guided and helped me move forward through my own grief and despair.

If you find one or two of these ways that resonate with you, practice them. Weave them into your everyday life and they will begin to take hold. Pay attention and notice any changes in yourself, and your surroundings.

This book is also about staying awake. I've slipped, forgotten, and fallen into old patterns, and each time, I'm reminded with a nudge and whisper to get back up. To stay awake to what matters and align with my soul's purpose. Let's not fall back to sleep. We need to stay awake! How do we keep from returning to an unawaken state? How are we to align with our souls and a higher calling?

You don't have to do it alone. There are many helpers in the Universe, rooting for you, wanting you to succeed and be joyful. You don't have to have a mystical experience to feel connected. Nor do you have to go to school for years to learn about it and earn a degree. You don't have to train to become a chaplain or end-of-life professional.

There is ancient wisdom available to us, saints and poets who have messages for our time, still speaking to us. Spiritual powers from across time and space. You carry this innate, primordial wisdom, too. You just have to tap into a deeper part of yourself to connect with it.

Perhaps these breadcrumbs can help you as you find a new way forward. There's a higher vibration on our earth beating now, one where we are being asked to tread softly, join the rhythm of nature, the seasons, and embrace our creativity, in whatever form that looks like.

I've included questions at the end of each chapter that may prompt reflection, journaling, or conversation with others.

It's up to each of us to step up and contribute our part. We each have a gift to share. Are you sharing yours? Your unique gift is one that is natural for you — it comes easily, yet you may brush it off. Often it gets covered up or hidden by roles we play and responsibilities we assume.

We aren't left on our own on this earth; rather, the divine is woven into all we do, in ways we don't often imagine. Heaven is not somewhere up in the clouds. It is right here among us on earth. Our mission then, is to lean into our lives, our deepest selves, embracing all our experiences — both the good and hard ones — to cultivate our unique gifts that we can share with others. Serving out of that place is the new heaven on earth.

After carrying around my divine visitation for nearly 20 years, I asked Spirit, *What do you want me to do?*

*Tell them who I am*, was the immediate answer.

Well, there you have it! This book is an attempt to do just that.

The poet Rilke writes about the beauty of getting older in his novel, *The Notebooks of Malte Laurids Brigge*,

"Ah, poems amount to so little when you write them too early in your life. You ought to wait and gather sense

and sweetness for a whole lifetime, and a long one if possible, and then, at the very end, you might perhaps be able
to write ten good lines. For poems are not, as people think,
simply emotions (one has emotions early enough) — they
are experiences."

Here are (hopefully) my ten good lines....

# 1

## GRACE

"Grace is the ability to redefine
the boundaries of possibility."
~Manning Marable

"Grace is the seed of resurrection
sown in our nature."
~Teilhard de Chardin

Life can change in an instant. I don't know about you,
but this was news to me. Evidently it's true, because
I'm living proof. Let me explain. My life changed
while driving to visit my dying father. He'd been diagnosed
with terminal lung cancer three months earlier and when I
left Durham, North Carolina, I was one person. But when
I got out of my car in Charlotte, I was another. Here's the
thing: I had a mystical experience on the way that changed
the course of my life. Seriously! It was crazy and I don't blame
you if you don't believe me.

Sometimes it's hard for me to wrap my brain around.

I was hurting and still reeling from my recent separation
from my disparaging husband and wasn't sure what the future
held for me. At this point, I didn't know anyone my age

who'd been through a breakup of their marriage. My friends were having their first babies, which was super hard on me. Others seemed to be thriving. I was not. At thirty-one years old, with my father dying, I was laboring my first divorce. Has anything like this ever happened to you? Everyone you know seems to be doing great, living their best life, and you're drowning in shit.

Plus, visiting my parents felt hard. My mother wasn't coping well at all with my father's pain and the fact that he wasn't getting better. It would've been nice if she could've been the grown up. For once.

"Oh, it's just so awful," she cried out one evening.

Reluctantly, I came home to help her as often as I could. My other three siblings all lived in other states.

What we didn't realize at the time is that my mother was already mourning my father's death. We all were. She was feeling what's known as anticipatory grief. Who knew there was such a thing?

Thanatologist Therese Rando, in her studies of the terminally ill, coined the term, "anticipatory mourning," referring to all the losses inherent in a life-threatening illness. The loss of dreams is one of the big ones and we tend to lug it around with us silently. We feel it when someone gets a dire diagnosis. One of the myths about grief is that it only *follows* a death. A reality that is rarely talked about, except among health-care professionals, is that grief can begin long before death happens.

Once death is on the horizon, even as a possibility, it's natural that we begin to grieve. Of course, we didn't know this was happening. If someone informed us, I didn't retain it.

"How did we get here so quickly?" I murmured.

Just seven months earlier, at Christmastime, my father compared the size of his legs for me while Pachelbel played in the background.

"See?" He pointed to his bony left one. The right leg was clearly twice as big as his left. "They can't find anything, but something's definitely not right."

Of course, I was concerned, anyone would be, and had been since he first noticed strange symptoms, but was distracted by mourning my failed marriage. My friends were celebrating the holidays with their responsible husbands and new babies, and I was jealous of their happy lives. Still, I was trying to enjoy my emancipation and my first Christmastide as a single woman. I've always learned things the hard way. This is how it works for me.

Then three and a half months later, right after Easter, during a routine appointment for monthly shots, my father's allergist noticed a large lump on his chest and sent him back to his general practitioner.

"You need to get that thing whacked off," his allergist urged. "It's not going away and important to find out what it is."

Dad was a competitive man by nature and often used sports metaphors. He referred to his primary physician, Dr. Hobson, as his quarterback. He ranked things as varsity for good; J.V. for not so good.

When Dr. Hobson called with the pathology report shortly after his subsequent appointment, my father knew the news wouldn't make either team. "He wouldn't be calling me if the results were good. I knew before he said anything."

"I'm afraid I have some very bad news," Dr. Hobson said to him.

The tumor turned out to be a carcinoma, a serious type of malignancy from an unknown source. Dad was immediately sent to Duke Medical Center to find and treat the aggressively growing cancer cells.

Dr. Moore, Dad's wise and good-humored oncologist at Duke, gave my 56-year-old father the dismal prognosis of terminal lung cancer, with six months to live and advised him to get his affairs in order. "It would be in your best interests to wrap up personal affairs that require concentration in the next six weeks," the doctor said.

A businessman, my father with German roots, liked German efficiency and punctuality — and German beer, preferably in a German beer stein. You get the picture. His grandfather moved his family from Aue, Germany to the United States before World War II and established a successful textile finishing machinery company in Worcester, Massachusetts.

My father's dad, my grandfather, in contrast, was an eccentric n'er-do-well, and while he attended the Philadelphia School of Textile and Design, he didn't last long working for the company. Instead, my grandfather collected miniature bronzed elephants, piddled around in his garden, drank toddies, and ended up dying in his late thirties. My father was only six when he lost his father to alcoholism. Shortly after, the elder Gessner, my great grandfather, died too, and his textile company was managed by a steward until my father finished school.

After graduating from Harvard Business School, my father stepped in and began running the David Gessner Company. With the industry failing in New England, textiles would eventually bring my family south to Charlotte, North Carolina, and Dad was set to run the American branch of a German company. But six months after relocating us, the Germans announced they were closing the U.S. operation and my father scrambled to buy them out.

I worked with him at Gessner Industries for three and a half years after college, partly to test out my interest in taking it over when my father retired. Being the only child of four who showed any interest in doing so, Dad remained hopeful. We traveled together all over the country, as well as internationally, to Milan and Paris for trade shows.

I managed the Gessner Industries booth for these events and talked about the naps of cloth, which is raised, fluffed fabric, like the inside of a sweatshirt, late into the evenings. This didn't particularly pique my interest, and while I met many interesting people, ate exquisite food, and drank expensive wine, it wasn't how I wanted to spend my days. Maybe you can relate. Marketing massive machines and spending half my time in the sweltering warehouses that housed them, was about as interesting as you imagine it might be. So painstakingly, I broke the news to my father that I didn't want to take over the company. I have a sneaky suspicion though; he already knew my heart just wasn't in it.

Dad had his flaws, but he's the guy you want around when you need life advice. He was the rational one of my parents, who always seemed to know what to do. My father was the backbone of our family, like an anchor, firmly attached to the earth. I could be safe with him in the world. With the anchor line being pulled, he was left drifting, and so was I.

I have a friend who said the most traumatic and transcendent things are those we don't see coming, we don't plan for. While I never really imagined my marriage would end so quickly, my friends did. I found out after our wedding, that some of them placed bets at the reception on how long we would last. Thinking back on that, I can only shake my head.

I kept hoping things would work out. *Oh, he'll get his act together,* I thought. *He won't rebel forever.* Deep down though, I knew it wouldn't last either.

My best friend, Debby, from Boston said over the phone, "Look, he's never going to change, okay? You just need to accept it and move on."

Something finally clicked inside, and I got it. I accepted reality and mustered up my nerve to leave my husband and new marriage behind.

I'm not sure if it was my relationship breaking up or Dad's terminal prognosis that split my heart open. I imagine it was both of those experiences colliding into each other that brought me to deep despair. My therapist at the time thought I intuitively knew before he was diagnosed that my father was really sick.

For instance, whenever my mother called, the news went from bad to worse. "His pain's increasing, they ran tests, can't find anything."

My heart sank. I dreaded her phone calls.

On this particular trip home, as I drove teary-eyed in the twilight, I panicked, *how in the world did I wind up here? How did my life end up like this?* This wasn't how I imagined my life would be when I was younger (as if it's anyone's). *What in God's name am I going to do?!*

In that very instant, I had an incredibly intense feeling that someone was in my car with me. So much so, that I whipped my head around to look in the back seat to see who was there. Of course, I was alone, but also, not-alone. I sensed something or *someone* with me — intangible, yet palpable and perfectly peaceful.

I was being held in the highest regard under a loving gaze. It was as if a benevolent, friendly Presence was looking directly into my soul and just bursting with love for me. (Ugh, I get it, you don't believe me. It's actually hard to write. But this is how it happened.) I felt enveloped, gathered in an embrace of empathy, almost cradled by an energy of unconditional love. There. I said it.

Although I couldn't visually see anyone, I felt an intense sense of communion with something big. A voice in my head spoke powerfully, yet reassuringly, and the message I heard lovingly and clearly was, "***You are not alone.***" Wow. That was exactly what I needed to hear.

The Persian poet Rumi described his mystical union as, "closer to me than myself to myself." This is the intimacy I experienced. And in that split second, I felt comforted.

Whatever was going on, I was completely entranced by this benevolent visitor. *What is happening? Is this God? A figment of my imagination? Could someone or something in the cosmos possibly be with me?*

Dazed, when I looked up and saw the dark road in front of me, out of the corner of my watery eyes, I caught a white speck of light in the rearview mirror. And there, I saw the biggest, yellowest, brightest, full moon I ever remembered shining in the night sky. It was as if that big, glowing ball was sitting there just for me, reminding me of the vast universe I was a part of, waxing and waning, and of the cycles of life.

And in that very moment, I felt ... a deep sense of belonging and connectedness. I was going to be okay, and maybe even more than okay, despite my devastating and embarrassing divorce, and in spite of my father's pending death. After all, it seems I wasn't alone.

*Ego Sum Noli timere.* "It is I, be not afraid." In that instant, I went from disconnected and drifting to feeling deeply connected to something larger than myself.

Now, we are, as you know, a skeptical people in these matters. And I'm totally open to the idea that this all happened in my head. That I was distraught, hating everything in the world, and that I imagined it. But here's the thing. If I did envision it, I'm in good company.

According to a Gallup poll, one out of three Americans has had a mystical experience. One out of three. Why don't we hear more about them? Because we live in a world of fear and judgment. I kept my mystical experience secret for far too long, until I couldn't anymore. What would happen if more of us let the cat out of the bag?

Julian of Norwich did just that. In the 14th century, she had an experience of Christ during the Black Death, a similar trauma to the global COVD pandemic, when half the European population died. Julian was gravely ill, in excruciating pain, and she thought she was dying, when suddenly, without any effort on her part, in her mind she heard words spoken to her by Christ.

"All shall be well, and all shall be well, and all manner of thing shall be well." St. Julian's words summarized her mystical visitation.

Julian was one of us. In the middle of a pandemic, the bubonic plague, her six-year-old son died. She was surrounded by death and illness, and yet, instantaneously felt love and peace after hearing words spoken to her by Christ. She heard the words clearly in her heart and mind. Julian's words provide a balm for our challenging times.

You know how you can feel unexpected sudden joy during a really hard time? Consequently, even in our happiest days, your heart can still weigh heavily for friends who are suffering.

Julian said her visions, her encounters with Christ, were not hers. Rather, they belong to all of us, to the human soul.

"They are ours, for we are all one," she realized.

The thing about a run-in with the divine is that you don't forget it. The memory is everlasting. In some ways, since that brief, magical encounter many years ago, I've spent my life seeking that union again. A shift happened for me in those moments and changed the course of my life.

While the whole thing probably lasted only a few seconds, it felt like a long, long time. It was a different kind of time, like when you're 'in the zone' or 'flow' and time seems to stand still. I was somehow restored and reconnected with a sense of well-being deep within, and it turned out to be a kind of awakening.

Although I wasn't a religious person, this direct exposure set me off on a pilgrimage of sorts, a peregrination as it's called in Celtic spirituality. I don't think this had to do with religion. There was no one stream or set of beliefs I needed to pledge to. My visitation was an invitation to personally connect with the divine, and the beginning of a path was revealed to me, some way I hadn't known before. I was navigating into radically new territory, and while I didn't choose this path, I didn't ignore it, either.

A path can consist of a collection of dirt, sand, stones, and grass. It includes everything – passion, curiosity, anticipation, and ignorance. Without those, you have no path. It's not smooth like a newly paved road.

Without much to lose, I chose to stay open to the brand-new ways and possibilities of living that I previously had no way of knowing. There's no reason why I should have been given this gift. It was only later that I realized what I received was grace, a freely given gift that reconnected me to my deepest identity.

And like Julian, I don't think this grace is unique to me. It's available to you, too. I just happened to be able to see it that evening. Who knows, maybe the timing was right, or I was ripe because of my then-dismal situation.

Celtic spirituality scholar, John Phillip Newell, says, "An experience of Presence is a song that is heard especially amid tears and confusion and brokenness. It's a melody that continues whether we are listening or not."

St. John, the beloved disciple of Jesus wrote, "Through tears we can see what clear-eyed we may otherwise miss." This is a theme in his writings. The mystical Gospel of John explores the way in which tears can open us up, instead of closing us down. Perhaps because I was grieving, I was more open to listening and accepting help.

You are not who you think you are. You are not left here alone on this planet to toil and figure everything out on your own. You are surrounded by a kind, invisible, yet vital life-force, who's got your back, gently pushing and pulling you toward your true center, your deepest identity. And once you become aware of that, everything becomes sacred. In some spiritual circles, this is known as ordinary magic.

Instead of assuming forks in the road, roadblocks, and blind alleyways are bad and frightening, what if you took the attitude that you can learn and grow from these detours, and stayed open to new ways appearing and being shown to you? The compassionate Presence in my car, that brief glimpse of an omniscient, divine source, the shining full moon, and the connectedness all contributed to my feeling a part of something new, beyond my family and current situation.

The Divine Presence grounding me in the midst of my anchor being pulled is none other than grace, and for some reason, I was able to reach out and take it. Even though it was a frightening and hopeless time, I felt peaceful knowing I wasn't alone and that I was now on a path to something bigger, something that felt like ... magic.

## Reflection Questions

I invite you to use the following prompts for reflection, journaling, or conversation:

- What are you currently grieving? Two important questions to ask yourself:

  - What am I learning from this experience?
  - Where is the universe or spirit working?

- Have you ever had a mystical experience? If so, how did it change you?
- What event(s) in your life split your heart open?
- When has life invited you to abandon the way that brought you to a specific point? How did this lead you toward a different path or new way of being?

- What helps you to remain open?
- St. Julian's words, "All shall be well, and all shall be well, and all manner of thing shall be well." How do these words land with you?
- Describe a time that you received grace, a freely given gift that supported you and restored your sense of well-being.

# 2

# EVERYDAY SAINTS

"This was love: a string of coincidences that gathered
significance and became miracles."
~ Chimamanda Ngozi Adichie, *Half of a Yellow Sun*

"In his holy flirtation with the world,
God occasionally drops a pocket handkerchief.
These handkerchiefs are called saints."
~ Frederick Buechner

The word was out, and my parents were besieged by well-wishers and friends. Jim Angler was a devout Catholic and branch manager at Merrill Lynch in uptown Charlotte, and my father's best friend. He stopped by to visit Dad every weekday during rush hour, on his way home from work. He'd rub and wash my father's swollen feet with water in a basin, while sipping a martini.

"This is how Jesus cared for his disciples," he shared one evening.

My father was a heavy drinker. When the textile industry started tanking years earlier, his drinking increased to relieve angst about money.

Once, during that period, my brother, David, and I got up the nerve to try a mini-intervention. With much trepidation, we told our father he needed to stop.

He looked at us deadpanned, and said, "I'd rather die than stop drinking."

Now, during one of Jim's visits Dad said, "The cruel joke is that now that I can drink whatever I want, I have no desire for it."

In fact, the only craving he had after chemo was hot dogs. My mother kept the grill on the back patio ready to fire up in case my emaciated father ever hungered for one. We'd take turns handfeeding him.

"It's clear the chemo isn't working, Heid," Dad reported during my visit.

He wasn't getting better – his right leg had shrunk so much it was the size of a young boy's. My heart shattered and I wanted to go back to the security of my mystical experience in the car. I was like a homing pigeon with the direct intent of reuniting with that safe, comforting union.

Simultaneously, serendipitous events bombarded me. I paid close attention to them. One of my closest high school friends called just when I was thinking of him. A song looping in my head suddenly came on the radio while I was driving. And my parents' friend, Susanne, handed me a book about grace, *Listening to Your Life,* by Frederick Buechner, a Presbyterian minister from Vermont.

Here's one of his relatable passages. "The grace of God means something like: Here is your life. You might never have been, but you are because the party wouldn't have been complete without you. Here is the world. Beautiful and terrible things will happen. Don't be afraid. I am with you. Nothing can ever separate us. It's for you I created the universe. I love you."

Buechner's writings spoke to a nascent part of me. I hung on every word and talked with Susanne about his writings and the numinous happenings around me. Like me, Buechner had a troubled family — he wrote about his alcoholic father, and how his dad and mother angrily and continually battled. Plus, he lived in New England, a bonus for me, having originated from there. If Buechner could find grace in his difficult past, maybe I could, too.

One day, Susanne invited me to go to church with her. The minister, Louis Patrick, was head pastor at Trinity Presbyterian Church, in Charlotte, and coincidently Buechner's close friend. They both studied at Union Theological Seminary in New York City and held open and progressive perspectives on a welcoming and relational God.

Years earlier, Lou had driven up to see Fred when he was going through a hard time with one of his children. His daughter was gravely ill, and he was frightened she might die. Lou got in the car and drove to Vermont from North Carolina.

He called Buechner on the phone to check in and Fred said, "How's the weather in Charlotte?"

Lou answered, "I wouldn't know, I'm calling from a phone booth one mile from your house."

Lou was a large, white-haired man, with a low, booming, God-like voice and hearty, full-bodied laugh. Think of Charlton Heston as Moses in the movie *The Ten Commandments* meets Santy Claus (as my grandmother, Nannie, liked to call him). Lou was likeable *and* a little intimidating and his sermons came alive for me — intelligent, profound messages, delivered with a quick wit and humor. His words made sense and were easily applicable to my current situation. It was as if he was speaking directly to me! For example, one Sunday he preached from the tall pulpit about how Jesus was a lighthouse who lit up the way and provided a pathway for us.

"Pay attention to that path," he pointed out.

Susanne wrote on the side of her bulletin; *Lou is my beacon*.

Susanne became mine and every week mailed me the cassette recordings of Patrick's soothing Sunday sermons.

"Read everything you can get your hands on," she suggested and gave me names of Buechner's other books. "Fred is to writing as Lou is to speaking and preaching."

A dynamic duo of sorts. Buechner dedicated his formative memoir *The Sacred Journey* to his companion. 'For Louis Patrick and all the other saints, remembered and forgotten, along the way.'

Susanne was the first living saint who took interest in me and accompanied me on my grief journey. She, coupled with the mystical, transcendent experience in my car, led me to an expanding worldview, beyond my troubled family. It was as if fresh air blew into my overwhelming feelings of what was happening to me, my father, and our family. Something shifted and despite the dark time, I felt buoyed with a nudge toward something new.

I just want to add a few thoughts here about saints: when you hear the word saint, images of extraordinary humans doing extraordinary things may pop into your head, like St. Francis with a couple of birds resting on his shoulders or St. Teresa wiping the brow of a dying leper in the streets of Calcutta. According to the Oxford English Dictionary, a saint is 'a very virtuous, kind, or patient person.'

"Oh, she's such a saint," you hear someone say about a person who's gone above and beyond to help another during a challenging time.

Here's the thing: The saints I've read about are passionate badasses. They're ordinary people who are living their lives the best they know how and connecting with a deeper part of themselves that hungers for expression. Their primordial selves tapped into the sacred resonance and their unique way of contributing something to this world. You have that in you, too. We all do.

Perhaps they were in a place because of their situation to become aware of Presence, the invisible force pushing or pulling them toward their true center. Your superpower or God-given talent may not look like theirs, but that doesn't mean it's not there, somewhere deep within you. We all can cultivate our individual gifts to contribute to the planet. A good thing, indeed!

In religious belief, a saint is a person who has an exceptional degree of holiness, likeness, or closeness to God. "He has the patience of a saint," you may have heard someone say. People who are spiritually adept have patience because they've realized that during a period of hardship there is often a nugget of learning or some blessing.

Have you ever noticed how some individuals step up during challenging times, and are not always the people you'd expect it to be? Friends you thought would've stayed by your side stepped back, while others, some acquaintances, materialized and came closer. Those are most likely your saints. Appreciate and accept their help. Who knows the underlying reason these people are showing up for you?

I had a friend once who told me about the "theory of thirds" during times of mourning. She said one third of individuals will neither help nor hinder your grief. Another third will make you feel worse simply by being around them. The last third will make you feel supported and loved. Why not seek out and hang around the latter third? You can often find these saints in a grief group setting. And if you're able, find a grief buddy, someone you can vent to who won't get tired of listening to you tell the same story over and over.

As layers of my father's ego got stripped away, so did his hair, his shape, his skills, and naturally he became more vulnerable. Dad was not a religious man, and I was surprised when he asked Susanne to set up a meeting for him with Lou. I can imagine what they talked about, although I don't know for sure. But when my father returned home, he seemed calmer, as if he checked off an important box on his final "to do" list.

"I used to be someone who went on business trips to Europe, ran Saturday errands to the hardware store, pharmacy and drycleaners, and mowed the lawn," my type-A father stated matter-of-factly. "Now the only task on my list is staying alive."

And as Dad got sicker and his world got smaller, just sitting with him quietly while he rested was enough. His personality had changed, and he'd become softer. Without his gruff exterior, another sort of beauty revealed itself, a beauty I imagine was the essence of my father.

It turns out the packaging is not who he'd been all along. The heart of my father wasn't about how many things he could check off his list. Who he was wasn't about *doing* at all. His underlying essence shone more brightly when the busyness was peeled away. Presence is more important than the roles we're so busy playing. Dying people, it turns out, can teach us this most directly.

The Buddhist Shambhala tradition uses the term "authentic presence" to describe people who are free of ego. There's a different feel about them, calmer but also more expansive. That expansion is their authentic presence. I witnessed this with my father, and later, over and over, in patients with life-threatening illnesses.

Religious traditions, both Western and Eastern, share a common iconography for this state: the halo. This is the symbol of authentic presence. But it's not just saints who manifest this radiance. You can discern it in everyday, ordinary people and things, for everyone has authentic presence. If you want to see it in art, look at Van Gogh's paintings, whether his stones, flowers, or living beings.

Another of my parents' friends introduced me to a book on quantum physics. The theory is that thinking isn't linear, but rather holistic, intuitive, and that quantum physics demonstrates that the universe is run on intention. This piqued my interest as this new, intuitive faith was burgeoning within me.

Growing up in the intellectual world of New England, you didn't talk about God. Nobody did. It was (and still is) embarrassing to use the word "God." And God forbid someone think I'm a "Jesus freak," associated with conservative fundamentalists, you know, the ones who fuel hatred and vote for the most conservative candidates. So, I stayed quiet.

Theologian Paul Tillich wrote, "We must let go of the word, 'God.'" Philosopher Martin Buber echoed this: "We must not let go of the word, God. God is our most primal word."

Evidently, I wasn't not alone in my struggle. Think of what the word and concept of God conjures up for you. It's been misused by so many people for so long, It wouldn't surprise me if God is a loaded word for you, too. It's also got bad associations for some secular cynics.

Someone at a mindfulness meditation retreat once told me that she can't even use the word God, and I understand that. It's hard for me to use the word God, but I want to. I want to connect to the ancient past, to our most primal word.

Here I was, mesmerized by this newly discovered, mysterious presence in the universe who took an interest in me and was guiding me. God, Spirit, Source, the Divine, Universe, Collective Consciousness, please fill in whatever word works for you. It grabbed a hold of me and woke up a part of me that was dormant.

I'd just like to add here how kind God is. And loyal. Seriously. Here I am unabashedly admitting I'm embarrassed to say her *name* after the unbelievable encounter I had! Some friend I am. Maybe you can relate. I'm not proud of it.

Here's the thing: Whatever that experience was of God (I'm going to use it!), I wanted more. I made up my mind to follow God, which was a road less traveled in my circles. My mystical, transcendent experience gave me the courage to take the leap of faith that granted me rebirth, a new beginning, perhaps a new life. You're more vulnerable when grieving, which makes you more malleable and open to change. I say that is a good thing.

Christ said, "You must die to be reborn." Maybe the moment in my car was something like that. Or at least the beginning of letting go of who I was or who I *thought* I was. Thus, the invitation began the process of allowing my psychological identity that I clung to, to be transfigured.

On one hand it was the hardest time of my life, but on the other, I felt more alive than ever before. Has this ever happened to you? For instance, I felt so connected to my dying father, who wasn't distracted by travel and work and making money. He was totally present, and I responded to that by leaning in, engaging with him and others, and paying attention, close attention to everything.

I also felt linked to Dr. Moore, my father's oncologist, and his medical team. They started to feel like family, and I was sad when we left Duke for the last time, knowing our developing relationship would end. I sorted through the mail when I was home just in case he'd sent a card.

My nurse friend, Kim, told me this is known as a "double loss," when family members not only face losing a loved one but the loss of their care team as well. The feelings can be interpreted as abandonment, which can evoke anger or hurt toward a physician or institution. You know how sometimes people want to sue the doctor or hospital, believing they caused their loved one's death? We thought about it for about one second when we looked back on how long it took to diagnose Dad, but let it go. Most of the time underneath that anger is grief.

Professional health-care providers mourn their patients and families with life-threatening illnesses as well. They develop close ties with their patients and family members, and this certainly happened with us at Duke. Perhaps it's happened to you, too.

Working in the hospital taught me that professional health-care providers' grief is disenfranchised, or unacknowledged, since it's not usually recognized and accepted by the medical institution. Since the bonding can be fast and intense, many providers experience a patient's pending death as personal and identify with the family's pain. This would've been good information to have, and I like to think Dr. Moore and his team thought of my father and us after we left the hospital that final time.

One last thing. The string of synchronistic happenings felt loosely strung together by a thin, gossamer thread. I was starting to see that thread more regularly, and it became sort of a lifeline. *Look for the sacred amidst the rubble*, somebody once said. All you have to do, is hang onto that thread, for dear life.

And sometimes if you're lucky, the everyday saints in your life — the Jim Anglers and Katharines and Lou Patricks — embody the gossamer thread. They too, are living, breathing, grace.

Years later, my spiritual director handed me a William Stafford poem about that very thing.

### *The Way It Is*

There's a thread you follow. It goes among
things that change. But it doesn't change.
People wonder about what you are pursuing.
You have to explain about the thread.
But it is hard for others to see.

While you hold it you can't get lost.
Tragedies happen; people get hurt
or die; and you suffer and get old.
Nothing you do can stop time's unfolding.
You don't ever let go of the thread.

## Reflection Questions

I invite you to use the following prompts for reflection, journaling, or conversation:

- What do you do when an unexplainable coincidence or serendipitous event happens to you?
- When grieving or going through a particularly challenging time, who stepped up to comfort you? How was this surprising, or not?
- Who are the everyday, living saints in your life?
- Do you use the word God easily? If not, what word do you prefer to use instead?
- What have been lifelines/threads for you amidst the rubble?
- Is there an author who accompanies you through life? One who you return to whose wisdom continues to speak to you? What is it in their words that is life giving for you?
- Where have you witnessed authentic presence in someone or something?
- Have you ever felt close to a health-care provider? Or felt a "double loss" when your contact ended? If so, what was it that made you feel connected?
- When have you felt grief that was disenfranchised or discounted?

# 3

## DAD'S DYING

"…how something returns and keeps on returning
through a gap, through a dimensional gate,
through a tear in the veil. And there it is again.
Another spring. To woo loss into song."
~Richard Schiffman, *Late March*

L ess than three weeks later my father walked out of the examining room at Duke, leaning on his cane with his eyes downcast.

"Dr. Moore is sending us home with Hospice," my mother gasped.

As my father would say, Hospice is a varsity service. As you may know, these saints provide care for individuals who have a life-limiting illness with a prognosis of six months or less to live. Their goal is to provide comfort measures that minimize or eliminate pain or other symptoms associated with the illness. Hospice care is wonderful at addressing the medical, emotional, social, and spiritual aspects of each person and his or her caregivers. This is amazingly accomplished through specialized services delivered by providers who are trained in end-of-life care.

Individuals who select Hospice care have chosen care that focuses on improving quality of life, physical, and emotional comfort, dignity, and peace of mind for themselves and their family. As great as this sounded, and as badly as we needed the physical and emotional care, I was still in denial that my father would die. *You don't know him,* I thought, *he's tough to kill. You'll see, he'll beat it.* Other friends have told me they thought the same thing about their dying family member.

So before enrolling in Hospice, we traveled to our summer home on Cape Cod, to celebrate July Fourth, and Dad's fifty-seventh birthday with friends, a lobster bake, and fireworks. It was an annual trip and my father wanted to visit one last time.

In years past, friends would stop by our cottage, welcoming us to the start of another summer, passing out little American flags to line our driveway, which was paved with crushed shells. During any other year, my dad would have snuck a trunkful of fireworks to New England, recently purchased from South Carolina. He would squeal with delight, like a little kid, lighting them on the dunes and rolling out of the way as they lit up the sky at the beach. On this trip, old friends came by to visit and pay their respects, and he skipped the dune rolling.

My mother tells the story of when they first bought our cape house. My older brother, David, was three years old and she would walk to the beach with me in a laundry basket with my brother running along beside her. Until the age of 20, I knew of no other place to be in the summer but on Cape Cod Bay. My first wedding was at the Chatham Bars Inn, on a low-tide beach with a full moon rising behind us.

Our deck overlooked Sesuit Harbor, where a steady stream of boats motored in and out all summer after passing through the jetties, which opens to the waiting bay. There were chaise lounge chairs with green and white striped cushions, a round patio table that housed a shaky umbrella, and old paint-chipped buoys hanging from the cedar shingles on the side of the house. Prominently placed were the halved whiskey barrels, which served as flowerpots for my mothers' beloved daises, red geraniums, and blue nasturtiums. It was always the first thing she worked on upon arriving to the cape house — even before unpacking.

*The Albatross*, one of the regular boats and a popular tourist sandy-bottom fishing rig, regularly returned at sunset, after the last trip of the day. My younger brother, Scott, worked on it for most of his teenage years. When I took my dirty clothes out to the shed to do laundry, there usually were piles of smelly and bloody one-dollar bills crumpled up on top of the dryer. They were Scott's tips from his day's work of scaling and fileting customers' flounders, complete with fish guts.

Captain Howes, who'd owned the boat since we were little kids, was now divorced with two daughters. He'd had a crush on my mother forever.

"I saw Dan Howes at the post office this morning," she'd announce girlishly. "That man has a twinkle in his eye."

My father liked order and tidiness, which showed in the care of his flagpole, which towered over our deck and held court over the harbor. Dad loved to collect flags and displayed one or more daily depending on his theme or mood.

"Achtung bitte!" he'd announce in German in the morning and then proudly raise the day's winners.

He had, to name a few, an American flag, Don't Tread on Me, North Carolina, a crimson Veritas Flag, the motto of Harvard University meaning - truth, kindness and beauty, and a Confederate Battle Flag that he would raise periodically to rile up and piss off the Yankee fishermen down at the harbor.

But my brother raised the flags for him on this trip. It was a confusing and heart-wrenching time at the Cape. After a couple of days, Dad asked to go home. His face was pale, jaundiced, and gaunt. He was tired. And he wanted to see his cat. The outer world no longer held much interest for him, which is common for individuals at the end of life. Their world becomes much smaller and what's going on inside becomes the focus, sometimes for the first time.

To be honest, I wanted to leave, too. It was painful to be there. I could see it in the eyes of our friends, as well. Plus, that ancient house wasn't set up for a sick person.

We went home to Charlotte and cocooned, thankful that Hospice would take charge. The nurse Kelly, who was assigned to us, was amazing in helping us with the transition. I made a mental note that once I got through all the craziness and exhaustion of this whole thing, I would check out what Hospice was all about. Whatever it was, I wanted to learn more. More about helping people and their families during this intense and rich time — it seemed right up my alley.

It would be some years before I would train as a chaplain and witness over and over how lucky my family had been to be under the care of Hospice. My father died at home in familiar surroundings, with all of us there, not alone in the sterile hospital environment.

Mom and I drove to the medical supply store to buy the hospital bed nurse Kelly recommended. You know how you think if you do exactly as you're told, everything will turn out okay? We bought just the right bed, and did what she said, but everything wasn't all right.

As my father increased his morphine boluses, we noticed he slept more and longer. At night, however, while we slept, he traded medication for pain to stay alert enough to write copious letters to us and his close friends, thanking us for our friendship and recounting funny times and stories. More than 20 years would pass before I learned that he even wrote to my college boyfriend, asking him to keep an eye out for me.

"I'll sleep when I'm dead," he stated dryly.

I read a wonderful line from Penelope Wilcock's *Spiritual Care of Dying and Bereaved People*: "When the people who we are with approach death, there is a sense of awe, the solemnity of a great moment approaching — a sacred moment."

The hot and sunny, southern July afternoon when he died was just that. My father was wearing his pajamas, not a hospital gown, and lying on the hospital bed we moved into his favorite room, the den. He had relaxed there and watched the Boston Celtics play and Jack Nicklaus win golf tournaments.

He was in a familiar place with a bay window where he could watch his birds splashing in their baths. Finches were dipping in and out to cool off from the late July southern heat. It was where my father's beloved Siamese, Mr. K, stalked these 'bookies' — the name my younger sister gave to birds as a toddler. A pregnant pecan tree drooped over the iron rod furniture with steady droppings of shells from satiated squirrels darting out to the end of limbs and back. The grill top was still open from the final time we grilled hot dogs — the last solid food my father could stomach, which would have mortified his healthier self.

He was surrounded by all of us and even had his cat, Mr. K, curled up on his hospital bed.

"I just don't want to lose my dignity," he had told us, and we remembered.

At four o'clock, Kelly told us when my father began "actively dying," and we stayed close to him, telling him we loved him as he slipped away. Kelly said my father was agonally breathing, which are the final breaths one takes when dying. They are sometimes referred to as the death rattle, because of the congested, scary choking sounds that often accompany them, and can sometimes go on for hours. We watched and waited for his last.

As Dad came in and out of consciousness, he began intentional and guttural breaths. His sucking inhalations were getting further and further apart, as he gasped for each breath.

I gestured for my mother to move in closer and take his grey-colored, lifeless hand. Then my father opened his eyes and let his head roll to his right side where my mother was leaning in, holding his hand. "I love you," he mouthed with his colorless lips.

"I love you ... it's okay ... you can go, we'll be all right," she whispered.

But we weren't all right. (Who is ever all right watching a family member die?) And then we realized he wasn't breathing anymore. Dad died at 5:00 pm, on a Thursday, which was serendipitously appropriate for my businessman father.

## REFLECTION QUESTIONS

I invite you to use the following prompts for reflection, journaling, or conversation:

- Reflect on a significant loss in your life. Were you present? What was that like for you to be there, or not be there?
- Who taught you about grief?

# 4

# FEATHER ON THE BREATH OF GOD

"Death ends a life, not a relationship."
~W.H. Auden

Grief brings you to the doorstep of learning. No one teaches you there are grief theories or stages or phases you'll go through. Grief felt messy, raw, and organic. It was unpredictable and terribly sad, and yet also kind of magical, an enlightening time. My best advice is to take the attitude that you're in new territory. Try it out. It just may ground you.

I walked around in an exhausted and disorganized fog. *Now what am I supposed to do?* I'd spent so much time caring for my father that I was at a loss for what to do with myself.

Life felt surreal. Upon waking each day, I was reminded, that indeed Dad was *dead,* and it was not a dream. Remember the movie with Bill Murray, *Groundhog Day,* when he keeps waking up and it's the same day? Imagine that kind of scenario.

I was annoyed that life went on, despite my father's death. Other people didn't seem to get the memo. When driving and waiting at a stoplight, I had strong urges to roll down my window and yell at the person next to me, "Don't you realize the world's changed? My father died!"

Author and spiritual teacher, Mirabai Starr, came up with these fabulous spiritual transformational stations for when you're grieving, based on Elizabeth Kubler-Ross's five stages of grief. I met this wise and beautiful soul years later when I attended her workshop, "This Beautiful Wound: The Mystics and Grief," at Holy Cross Monastery in upstate New York.

Mirabai is a mystic scholar and writes contemporary translations of sacred literature. She taught our group of retreatants that the sixteenth century Spanish saint, Teresa of Avila, speaks of 'the beautiful wound' of longing for God, describing this depth of suffering as a "doorway to union with her Beloved." Mirabai helps mourners harness the transformational power of loss through writing and sees the "ravaged landscape of our lives as holy ground."

This was music to my ears.

Mirabai says we go through different grief portals that offer us the opportunity to transform. I think she'd say I was pulling into the anger portal. In this transformational station you're saying to the world, "This is not okay!" You see things as you want them to be, not as how they are, which Buddhists say is the cause of suffering. Your feelings can range from irritation to rage.

For instance, say your partner is chewing, eating cereal, and crunching loudly with an open mouth and slurping the milk. This might drive you over the edge. You may be struggling very hard not to say something mean. You consider leaving this person who chews so annoyingly. But you might also consider just trying to breathe in that moment. You're more reactive in this grief station and little things bug you more than usual.

My mother was a mess. I took family leave from my job and accompanied her back to Cape Cod. She'd fallen into a deep depression and didn't like being alone. David and I thought if Mom spent some time in her favorite place near the ocean, she might snap out of it. David was back in Colorado where he'd been living, so I traveled to the Cape (as we called it) with our mother, alone.

I'd never seen my mother like this. She could barely get dressed in the morning and had no energy to do anything. Normally, she'd lunch with her friends, play golf, paint, and plant her window boxes, filling her halved whiskey barrels on our deck with pink geraniums and purple nasturtiums. She did none of those things.

It freaked me out. I didn't see this coming. We always knew Dad wouldn't fare well if Mom died first, but we secretly thought Mom would thrive. Or maybe we covertly wanted this.

Let me tell you a quick story. Many years ago, my mother went to see a psychologist that one of her friends recommended. After hearing mom's story, her therapist told her that if she didn't start dealing with her issues, she was headed for a major depression. When Mom told me this (which very well may be a boundary issue in itself), I couldn't imagine that ever happening to this woman.

My mother was a social dynamo — chair of the Mint Museum Gala, Junior League President, trophies proudly displayed on our mantel from her country-club golf and tennis tournaments won, and our telephone always ringing off the hook for invitations somewhere. All of this with her ever glowing bronzed Danish skin from her latest trip with my father.

"Why would I want to talk about and relive those things?" was my mother's response to her therapist's admonition.

To make a long story short, Mom didn't go back to her therapist and buried her bad times. She pretended they never happened because they were too hard to deal with, too unsettling to remember. Don't let this be you.

The problem with not looking at things, is that they don't go away. Your ignored issues live on in your body and mind and fester. They often come out sideways in unwanted behavior and anger. How often have you seen that, someone bites your head off for no good reason, only to find out they were triggered by a reminder of a lingering, unresolved matter and extra sensitive about it.

There are two hard-won gifts for doing your grief work and given the sacrifice, they better be good ones. Luckily, they are rich offerings: wisdom and increased compassion. My mother paid a price for not dealing with her stuff because a certain part of her stopped growing in those directions. Ironically, your deepest wounds can be a place of strength if you can learn from and integrate them. This is what many of the saints did so well.

It's hard work, right? Who wants to do it? But in the end, if you can face your challenging issues and do some work around them, rather than resist them, you build resilience. And eventually you may be surprised to find that when something triggers you, you're not as reactive.

And wisdom is such a vital gift, it's a shame to miss out on it. Celtic spirituality author John Phillip Newell rewrote passages of Scripture for his prayer book *Celtic Treasure*. Here's an excerpt of his Proverbs 8:

Wisdom calls us from the crossroads of life.

She raises her voice and says:

"To you, O people, I call. My words are to all who live.
Come to me, you who lack understanding.
Hear, for I will speak gracious things and from my lips will come what is true and right.

Seek my teachings instead of silver and my
knowledge rather than gold for wisdom is better
than jewels and everything else you desire does
not compare with her.
I, wisdom, will offer you awareness and strength
of soul.
I walk in the way of right relationships and along
the paths of peace...."

My favorite line is, "I, wisdom, will offer you awareness
and strength of soul." I missed my father and wished he
were around to help me and my mother, especially with the
strength part.

I became fascinated about *where* he was. My siblings,
mother, and I had all gathered around his hospital bed in
our den when his yellow face dropped to the side as he took
one last sucking inhalation. We waited for another breath,
but it didn't come. His mouth was still partly open. One
thing I knew at that time — my father was no longer lying
in that bed.

After he died, someone took his body out of our house
to a funeral home. Dad was cremated and his remains were
put into an urn. But *he* was gone. Gone where? Where was
the *essence* of him?

In the Celtic tradition, after a death, a window is opened
to allow the spirit of the deceased to leave the house. No
one can stand or block the path to the window as this may
prevent the spirit from leaving. *And to go where?* We didn't
open a window. *Did his spirit stay in our house?*

I believe my father was free from struggling — from air
hunger and from pain. His aura, his spirit, was released. Some
religions believe we return to the light we originally came
from. From light you came and to light you shall return.

I think he went back to the light.

We sprinkled his ashes in his favorite spot, into the bay near our family home on Cape Cod. He had spent many long summer days there on his boat, *Sea-Ges*, with family and friends. The bay seemed the perfect place for him to hang out for eternity.

As I lay in bed upstairs in our Cape house, the mourning doves greeted me upon awakening, with their lamenting, haunting cries, as if in solidarity with me. Their familiar coos had been there my whole life, but since my mysterious encounter, I was more attuned to listen and look for Presence. I paid more attention now.

You know how you've heard some sounds your entire existence and not really noticed them, until one day you really hear them in a new way? Then when you get wind of them again in a different place they're comforting. When I hear mourning doves now, no matter where I am, fond memories of Cape Cod summers come to mind.

Here's another example: During the fall season on Sundays in our house growing up, football was on the television, mainly the Patriots. My father and brothers glued themselves to the tube for these games. While I never really watched any of it, the blowing whistles and commentators calling plays and their remarks were a customary hum in the background.

Years later when I was on my own, it dawned on me that I actually missed hearing those familiar sounds. Sometimes I'd turn on and tune into the comforting noise of NFL Sunday even though I didn't watch. In his early teens, my son Noah became a Carolina Panthers fan, and the Sunday routine began again. Maybe you can relate or have your own version of this.

I wrote in my journal, *The Holy One sends me birds, mourning doves, to remind me I am not alone. She is near. I'm not alone!* Doves have long since been associated with myths, folklore, and religions. In Slavic folklore, doves were believed to accompany the souls of the dead to heaven. In Muslim lore, a dove murmured the words of God into the ear of Muhammad. For the Celts, the mournful call of a dove meant the peaceful passing of someone. A friend of mine added that mourning doves call out to their loved one who is gone.

As a symbol of the Holy Spirit, the dove is associated with the mystical fifth element of spirit. Of course, the dove nowadays is a symbol of peace. They call you to regain your serenity. The dove reminds you to take a deep breath and release tension and stress.

Years later I would add barred owls, Canada geese, cardinals, and beloved blue herons to my list. These birds lifted me up out of the paralyzing grief grip and symbolized the liminal space and connection between two worlds.

The biggest relief in those early days were my daily walks. I walked everywhere — long strolls along the length of the beaches, or sandy, paved roads, down dirt-covered Paddock's Path, or across slippery seaweed-covered rocks below the cliff at Stone's Mansion.

One day as I headed out for my hike around the neck, as it's known, I was distraught after being in our cottage with my depressed mother all morning. Her listlessness was scaring me, and I ran out of the house for some air, to clear my head. As I turned the corner from our home onto Sesuit Neck Road, there in front of me I saw a tiny, beautiful, baby-blue feather, gently lying there, as if for me. *"All shall be well, and all shall be well, and all matter of thing shall be well,"* St. Julian's words echoed in my head. I felt immediate relief and comfort and took it as a symbol of encouragement.

Mourning is exhausting work, and this little billowy feather inspired me; it was life-giving. Feathers started appearing just when I needed a shot of hope. Reminders that some sort of caring presence was close by, looking out for me.

More than anything since that visit, the feathers were reminiscent of the healing, ethereal whisper I heard in my car.

They were little intuitive nudges saying, "You're okay, you're on the right path, keep going." I found them almost daily that summer, in every remote corner of the neck I walked.

Feathers became my little support team, cheering me on and reminding me I wasn't alone. That there was more going on beneath the surface. I was experiencing the deeply personal nature of the universe. These glimpses of grace buoyed my sense of well-being and became my personal portal to the Sacred.

And I was scared. I felt responsible for my mother's well-being now that Dad was gone. Often feeling overwhelmed, I'd run out for my walk. My solace and respite might be a little owl feather lying at my feet. Feathers are silent, and I'm struggling not to use the word tranquility here, but that's the feeling they brought, a quietude.

At first, I thought it was my father, letting me know he was okay. In many cultures, feathers represent a connection to the spiritual realm, and are a symbol of the soul. In the Celtic tradition, a vernicle is a symbol of travel to a sacred place. Feathers became my vernicle. They had a silent way of stopping me in my tracks and delighting me enough to pick them up, take with me and add them to my collection at home.

I always thought I'd remember the circumstances surrounding their appearance, but never did, so started taping little Post-it notes to them to remember.

Even still, I couldn't quite recapture the feeling. One morning I journaled,

Baby feather at my feet
quietly reminding me all is well.
Once again surprised, I smile and pick it up
suddenly remembering there is more than meets the eye.
For fear and worry are fleeting,
yet a nudge from beyond, eternal.

I carry on trying to capture this knowing in my soul,
though I'll forget, as I do,
until the next time I need reassurance.
Then I'll be met again with a simple comforting gift
of the present.

Years later I went to see a consciousness educator, who was part psychic and part telepathic communicator. My tennis friend, Kim, met with her and said she was amazing. *What if what she tells me is bad?* I made an appointment anyway.

Tomiko worked at Duke University in the paranormal studies department. When I sat down on her well-worn sofa in her tiny apartment, Tomiko instructed me to write my first name in script and to list five more first names. She didn't ask me anything about myself or my family. I wrote my name and five others, one of which was my father's. She took the small thin notebook paper from me, folded it, and held it tightly in her hand. Then Tomiko ran her fingers over my name and each of the following ones.

"I know why you came to see me," she shared, halfway through her discourse on my life and its trajectory. "It's because of your father. Let's speak to him and see what he has to say."

Tomiko was silent for several minutes, her eyes closed, holding my little, wrinkled paper tightly with both hands.

Suddenly her mannerisms changed and seemed familiar. Her voice deepened and took on my father's tone and inflection. She even scratched the back of her neck the way he did when he was thinking.

Finally, she spoke. "I'd like to be your helper. I am evolving. Pray for me. You're the only one who believes I'm still here. Think of me when you are reading something exciting. Call my name. Imagine you are speaking to my spirit or my mind ... I want to be helpful to you ... I love you."

"Where are you, Dad?!" I blurted.

"I am exactly where you are, how about that? Keep me alive. I want to be useful, so, you keep me alive. I love you."

I couldn't have anticipated that moment and wasn't really sure what to do with my encounter with Tomiko, but it did reflect what I needed to hear at the time. My Dad's message to me through Tomiko was the most beautiful feather I'd found yet. I love that.

## REFLECTION QUESTIONS

I invite you to use the following prompts for reflection, journaling, or conversation:

- When have you wanted to yell at the world for moving on?
- When have you felt extra compassion for someone grieving something you've experienced?
- What are the things for you that are gentle reminders of fundamental truths, that "all is well," even if you don't necessarily feel that way?

# 5

## TRUSTING THE PATH

"Even if one glimpses God, there are still cuts and
splinters and burns along the way."
~Mark Nepo

"The intuitive mind is a sacred gift and the rational
mind is a faithful servant. We have created a society
that honors the servant and has forgotten the gift."
~Albert Einstein

I met my second husband, Matt, at a party. I was rocking
Jacob, the baby of my friend, Mary Ann, on the front
porch of the old farmhouse, when Matt struck up a
conversation. The next morning, my friend, Judy, told me
someone from the night before was asking about me.

I later found out that when Matt saw me cradling Jacob,
he said to a friend, "That's who I want to be the mother of
my children."

I was separated at the time, worried about my father, and
hungry for some male attention. I wanted to feel pretty. Matt
seemed the opposite of my first husband, Bill. He didn't drink
alcohol and had a calm temperament. He was kind and gentle

in nature. When I brought him home for the holidays, my mother called him a 'Christmas miracle.'

I liked Matt as a friend, but wished it was in a more romantic way. He adored me and was healing for my bruised ego. I wanted babies with someone nurturing and supportive. Plus, he owned his own business and was a hard worker.

I wasn't in love with Matt, but I was hopeful I *could* fall in love with him. So even though a steady whisper in my gut pulsed "no," out of fear, I ignored it and moved forward.

His mother, Ellie Mae, said, "If Matt hadn't met Heidi, I don't think he would've ever gotten married."

I broke up with Matt once, but later, when he showed up at my father's memorial service, I was touched. So, in the midst of my grief-stricken loneliness after Dad died, I reached back out. I was tired of struggling alone.

Author C.S. Lewis tells us in his memoir *A Grief Observed*, "Nobody told me grief feels so much like fear."

Grief knocks you off your center, it's unpredictable, and 18 months after my father died, I married Matt in a small ceremony in the mountains of North Carolina. I delivered our son nine months later. My therapist, Lauren, thought I married Matt to have my children. I think she may have been right. Matt and I made two beautiful humans, Noah and Adeline.

I wish my hope for us had manifested, but sadly, it didn't. I took a chance and willed myself to fall in love him, or at least with the hopes of growing into love, but except for a few isolated incidents, that didn't happen.

At our ceremony, my father's best friend, Jim Angler, the saint who had washed my father's feet while drinking martinis, advised us to join a church and get involved.

"Stay connected to it," he stated. "A cord of three strands is not easily broken."

I heeded his advice and started looking around for one. I found a Presbyterian church we both agreed on. Secretly, I hoped to catch another whiff of the God who found me in my Honda, so jumped in with two feet and got involved. I was on the session committee, which was the backbone of the church; volunteered in the nursery; and chaired the social activities committee.

The people I met at that little church were wonderful. They were welcoming and caring. I just didn't find anyone who'd had an experience similar to mine, or maybe they were hiding theirs, too. I didn't feel comfortable enough to share my mystical experience.

The thing is, the God and Jesus I heard about at church didn't *feel* like the divine presence I experienced. There was a clear disconnect. The church was all so heady and intellectual. I was doing all the right things and in the right place, but wasn't spiritually nourished. (Incidentally, there seemed to be a parallel with my husband, Matt. I thought I correctly chose this time, that I was doing the right thing, but we weren't connecting.)

I craved connecting with the mystical, transcendent Spirit who brought *ruah*, the breath of fresh air, like Ehecatl, the Aztec God of air and winds. I did not feel this in church. There was community there, but my heart yearned for the deeply personal and slightly mysterious Holy One.

So, I started looking around again. Peace and quiet was important. Every time I sensed a Holy Presence, it was in stillness. The Persian poet Rumi said, "God's language is silence. Everything else is poor translation."

I also experienced this transcendent connection in nature. A Muslim friend of mine told me that nature is the soul of God and has a consciousness, so speak and act lovingly. Have you ever noticed how you don't feel alone when you're in the natural world? Nature and meditation are two places where one can feel unity.

I started attending contemplative evening prayer services at the Holy Family Episcopal Church, recommended by my therapist, Lauren. I had sought Lauren out when I knew my marriage with Bill was over. I needed to get in a healthier emotional place to leave him. We'd only been married two years but were not a good match. We both needed something very different from what we could give each other and should've remained just good friends.

Lauren introduced me to Episcopalian Contemplative Prayer. She was very involved with these prayer services at her church and shared that sometimes she meditated in her home office for hours at a time. To borrow a line from writer Anne Lamott, "I started to worry that a nice long discussion of aromatherapy was right around the corner."

But she was onto something.

Contemplative Prayer is like meditation but has a spiritual component that will ground you in relative silence. I started attending these services at Lauren's church. I'd arrive a little before 6:30 in the evening to help light the candles and sit with a handful of people in silence for 25 minutes. The 'sits' opened with a prayer and ended with a reading or two, usually a psalm or short passage.

Quiet companionship with strangers is peaceful and restful. I felt nurtured and spiritually fed. There is an intimacy fostered by shared silent prayer.

The opening prayer helped me drop below my worries of the day:

> *Come to us, Holy Wonder, as we gather.*
> *Encircle us with your love.*
> *Bless us with your sustaining presence.*
> *Surround us with your grace.*

*Draw us 'round your living word.*
*Bind us to one another and to you. Amen.*

This contemplative way drew me in and led me toward the desert fathers and mothers. One of those was the 16<sup>th</sup> century Christian Mystic Saint Teresa of Avila, from Spain. This 'beautiful wound' saint was a passionate reformer of the church. She founded a home for Discalced, or barefoot, Carmelites, wearing only the humblest of sandals made from hand-woven hemp as an emblem of simplicity.

Teresa reminds me of Stacey Abrams, the fervent American politician, lawyer, and voting-rights activist, who rallies and fires up people around social-justice issues. I imagine they have the same energy, or vibe, as my daughter would say.

In her book *The Interior Castle,* Teresa recounts her mystical vision from Christ in which he showed her the soul as a brilliant crystal palace, from the center of which the Beloved is beckoning the lover to merge with him. She recounts that all you have to do to be with God, is to close your eyes and go within.

Mystical scholar Mirabai Starr wrote a contemporary translation of Teresa's book, as well as *Dark Night of the Soul,* written by her favorite saint, John of the Cross. Saint Teresa was his mentor and he joined her and her Carmelite sisters to reform the corrupt church of its many rules and regulations.

But John was soon taken prisoner by adversaries and locked up in a tiny cell. John endured an impossible time, confined in isolation, and descended into the depths of darkness. Despite this grim reality, he embraced two powerful allies that provided solace during his captivity -- writing poetry in his head and watching the stars above him at night, through a small opening in the roof of his wooden cell. St. John developed a teaching on how one can surrender themselves to 'the divine' by allowing deep sorrows in life to be seen as a spiritual blessing from which we grow, rather than burdensome problems needing solutions.

I related to the mystics. These were my people and comforted me across space and time.

A call to study theology and chaplaincy bubbled below the surface. I'd had meaningful discussions while at Duke Hospital with my father, in waiting rooms with other families, and with staff, about what they were feeling and experiencing. I felt relatively comfortable talking about dying and death and found the compassionate conversations to be genuine and deep.

One evening at Holy Family church before prayer, I heard someone talking about a class being offered, *Education for Ministry* (EFM). EFM is a four-year, interdenominational course of group study that provides a framework to connect faith to daily life through reading and discussion. The program has concentrations in the Old and New Testaments, church history, and theologian study. Along with the academic component, the program is geared to help participants discern a call to ministry, so I enrolled. I had questions about my burgeoning faith.

Meeting once a week with a group led by a mentor, you learn how to think theologically and articulate your faith. My group included our young leader, who was also a mother, and recovering from her conservative, evangelical background; a University of North Carolina communications professor and her entrepreneur husband; an elderly, retired couple; a young female high-school teacher; and a couple my own age with small children.

This open-minded group taught me a lot, *and* I have to say, was very heady. I was surprised more in the group hadn't had a mystical experience. That *was* my theology.

As one of the participants said, "It's as if God grabbed a hold of you and won't let go."

Our service to the church was performing evening prayer twice a month. We rotated responsibility for conducting the worship service, and I looked forward to attending, as well as preparing and presenting liturgy. This intimate time connected us deeply to each other. Though we didn't really socialize outside of class time, I often felt that I knew them better than just about anyone I'd ever met.

One of the couples in our group were Nowell and Jennifer. Their daughter and son played in the nursery with my children while we were in class. Nowell is one of those people in your life who makes an impact, even though you haven't known each other for long. He was the saint who taught me to trust my gut.

Nowell pointed out, "I don't do things if it doesn't feel right in my belly. I wait until I want to do something, when I get the energy. Then it's easy."

Isn't this the coolest thing? It aligned with my intuitive faith that was developing. When you're not sure if you want to do something, you get quiet and try to hear that still small voice inside. Listen for what it tells you to do or not to do.

The challenge is that so many of us stopped trusting it as children. When we listened to our intuition when we were small and then told grown-ups what we believed, we were often corrected or laughed at.

Like me, you may have gotten into the habit of doubting the voice that was telling you quite clearly what was really going on. I started thinking everyone else knew more than I did. Everyone *outside of me*. But they don't know what is best for me, or for you, and it's important that you get it back.

You retrieve it by trusting yourself, and being on your own side, even when you do it poorly at first. Train yourself to hear that small, inner voice. It may take some practice, but you can do it. Start with small things, like perhaps what restaurant you want to go to when eating out with friends or family.

Maybe this sounds familiar. "Where do you want to go for dinner?"

"I don't know, where do you want to go?"

"I don't know."

I sensed Nowell and I were kindred spirits, and I've carried his lesson with me ever since, although I admit not always following through on a nudge or inkling. Little did I know I'd be officiating Nowell's 'green' graveside service after he died of prostate cancer, nearly 20 years later.

All those years later, I was in line at the Harris Teeter Grocery Store, when someone behind me called my name. It was Jennifer and when we got out into the parking lot she updated me on Nowell's life-threatening diagnosis, "We're hoping the radiation and chemotherapy will contain the cancer."

Sadly, it didn't and the aggressively moving malignant cells spread throughout Nowell's husky frame. I got a call from Jennifer asking me to officiate his memorial service when the time came.

On a Friday evening toward the end of his life, Jennifer and their three teenagers hosted a "drop in" at their house for friends to come and visit with Nowell. He wanted to see his people one more time, and like my father, say good-bye and thank them for their friendship. This is an important exchange for someone who is dying and for those being left behind. It's a gift that can bring closure and comfort, as well as the opportunity for any last words.

As I held Nowell's grey hand, and sat on the side of his hospital bed, prominently placed in their dining room, I gratefully recounted the gift he gave me all those years ago of trusting my intuition, and how much that impacted me. "I think of you every time I trust my gut."

"Thank you for sharing that with me, Heidi," his colorless lips mouthed.

After Nowell died, his family kept his body on that hospital bed in their dining room for three days. It may sound strange but being with a dead body can help focus your mind on your mortality and on the preciousness of what time you have left. Some Buddhist practices encourage monks to sit with dead bodies, sometimes for several days. And in many Christian monastic communities, the members sit in vigil with the body of a monastic brother or sister who has died. This vigil is both a sign of respect for the one who has died and a lesson for those who are still alive.

The morning of Nowell's service, I stumbled upon a large, barred owl's feather lying on the ground just outside my car door. I had a sneaky suspicion it was from Nowell. Jennifer told me he had a thing with feathers as well, and I will forever equate owls with Nowell.

In many cultures, to see or hear an owl is an omen of death. In ancient Greece, however, owls were associated with Athena, the goddess of wisdom, and were considered lucky. And in ancient Egypt, the owl hieroglyph represented the letter M and symbolized wisdom, mystical goddess-related knowledge, and secrets, all associations still commonly made with the owl today.

The owl reminds you to trust your own wisdom and intuition, and to trust yourself in a time of uncertainty. This seemed an appropriate bird totem for Nowell. Next time you hear an owl, take note of what's happening in your life.

Nowell was buried in a pine box and lowered into a deep hole dug by his friends and family on his buddy's farm. It was a beautiful fall afternoon and throughout the service scores of people paid tribute to him. Nowell and Jennifer were musicians and hand-crafted violins for a living, owning their own shop.

Jennifer shared with me Nowell's saying when he had a violin repair hanging over his head. "Sometimes you just have to wait for the moon to be right."

Fiddlers played bluegrass and singing filled the air as we laid Nowell to rest with la Luna rising to just the right spot.

## REFLECTION QUESTIONS

I invite you to use the following prompts for reflection, journaling, or conversation:

- Name a time when you followed your gut, or intuition. When didn't you even though you knew you should have?

# 6

## TRANSFER STUDENT

"Dawn comes with the cry of the wild goose."
~Kenneth White

"In all things of nature,
there is something of the marvelous."
~Aristotle

After two years of Education for Ministry, I sought out a spiritual director. Spiritual directors are trained people who help you see where God is working in your life. They help you pay attention, which naturally cultivates awareness of your surroundings. They also help you pay special attention to God and where she might be moving. In the Celtic Christian tradition this is called the *anam cara* relationship — a conversation partner whose presence and holy listening calls forth what is stirring in your depths, longing to come up into consciousness.

Karen was the perfect spiritual director for me. She lived in what seemed to be a little tree house, and we'd meet in her "basement" surrounded by windows and birdfeeders. Typically, you meet monthly to leave time for Spirit's movement. I met with Karen, once a month, for nearly 25 years, and she helped me articulate and navigate whatever was bubbling beneath the surface.

"Tell me about how you're praying these days," she'd question.

My response never wavered much, "Oh, it's like an ongoing conversation."

Karen pushed me for details.

She was a psychologist by profession and worked at Duke as a researcher. Karen also trained at The Shalem Institute, for her spiritual direction certificate. The Shalem Institute centers on contemplative teaching and practices that open the mind and awaken the heart to the living Spirit. I especially loved that this contemplative spirituality drew from the wisdom of many religious traditions.

It became clear from our conversations that my spiritual awakening pointed to hospital chaplaincy. As a hospital chaplain, I'd be a familiar face for people who were confronted with frightening situations in a large, unfamiliar place. I'd help them navigate the strange and scary world of the hospital, because no matter the reason you're there — a broken arm or a life-threatening illness — if you're in a hospital, it's stressful. The hospital is a place I could live out my message, "You are not alone." I didn't want to take care of people as much as connect them with resources and this deeper wisdom I was learning.

One evening during this time when our kids were little, my husband, Matt offered to give our daughter, Addie, as we called her, a bath and I grabbed the opportunity for a walk by myself. I headed for the door, and didn't even take my dog, Sam, with me, which was unusual.

As I turned the corner into the next familiar neighborhood, the sidewalk looked like a fairytale walkway, with the trees curved toward each other, creating an archway, a green tunnel for me to pass through. Since the Cape trip when I started finding feathers, walks were a regular thing. On this evening, I briskly walked off the day's stress and worries, luxuriating and basking in my solitude.

Suddenly, out of nowhere, I heard what sounded like a large bird flapping its wings vigorously and loudly above me. Although I couldn't see anything, the flapping of wings was getting louder and closer. It seemed to go on for a couple minutes. I crouched down and crossed my arms over my head for protection, fearing it may nosedive into me. As I turned my head upward to locate the bird, nothing was there. The screeching stopped, and absolutely nothing was there, except for lots of feathers at my feet.

*What was that?! An owl... Dad?* As surprising and scary as this experience was, it also felt exciting — wild and organic. I longed to tell someone about what just happened. Nowell and his wife, Jennifer crossed my mind.

I kept walking and ran into the only other friend in the world who wouldn't think I'd lost my mind. Bev was the perfect person to share this with. She worked as a nurse in the pediatric intensive care unit with really sick children. Bev also led poetry classes for the nurses who cared for them.

Years later when I became a chaplain, Bev was focusing more on her passion of creating art and became a botanical illustrator. I hired her to design the condolence cards for the University of North Carolina Hospitals Bereavement Support Service, as well as other special projects. She lived in the neighborhood, and we often walked together along this path.

"You're not going to believe what just happened to me!" I blurted out.

Bev was intrigued and finished the walk with me. "Did you know feathers symbolize the soul?"

I didn't know what to do with that experience and besides Bev, kept it to myself. Only recently have I read and heard of others who've had similar experiences. There's even a name for what I believe happened to me. It's called a "walk-in," or "transfer student."

The theory is that when the soul in the body becomes disillusioned with life and wants out, another soul, often an advanced being, enters the body. An agreed-upon exchange takes place. Usually, the new soul has something of great value to bring to the world. The consciousness of a transfer soul is always higher than the original soul in the body, and this can be either a temporary or permanent exchange.

Now, stay with me here. This seems far-fetched, even to me, and I have no idea if it is true. Who's to say? Either way, it's probably just as well I didn't know about this explanation at the time.

Matt's small oil-recycling business was struggling to stay afloat. He was competing with giant, national oil companies. Money was tight and I had my hands full with my two young children, Noah and Addie. Matt was preoccupied with keeping the business going and I needed money for the kids and to keep our house running.

Our marriage was strained, and when I got scared and overwhelmed, day or night, I started to hear, out of thin air, a gaggle of geese fly above me or over our house, honking as they flew by. I imagined they were heading to the neighboring pond, and was immediately relieved, breathing in, *all shall be well, and all shall be well, and all manner of thing shall be well.* The geese became my friends, their supportive honking a greeting. There was a numinous quality to their unannounced visits.

The poet Mary Oliver reminds us in her poem *Wild Geese:*

> "Whoever you are, no matter how lonely, the world
> offers itself to your imagination, calls to you like
> wild geese, harsh and exciting — over and over,
> announcing your place in the family of things."

Years before I read this poem, in those moments, I knew those geese were calling for me! In Celtic spirituality, geese symbolize the Holy Spirit. The geese were still watching over me when I left Matt a few years later.

Often at my most lonely and frightened as a single mother, not sure how I'd pay our rent, honking geese would pass over our townhouse. Dawn or dusk, the moment I felt panic, there they were, "honk, honk, honk!" A smile and deep sigh of appreciation was my response. *Thank you for the reminder...* I'd exhale. I'd forget, and frightened another time, they'd show up again like clockwork. Their helpful reminders kept me moving forward.

## REFLECTION QUESTIONS

I invite you to use the following prompts for reflection, journaling, or conversation:

- What are the little reminders that keep you grounded amidst life's challenges?
- When was the last time you had a deep connection in the natural world?
- Do you have a conversation partner who helps you discern what's happening in your life? If so, what is it about that relationship that is satisfying for you?
- What aspects of your life are still hard for you to share with another person?
- How hard is it for you to be vulnerable with another person?

# 7

# CHAPLAIN SCHOOL

"How we decide to live our lives at the most
trying of moments — is it going to be
a wasteland or is it going to be a grail quest?"
~Joseph Campbell

"Vocation is the place where your deep
gladness and the world's deep hunger meet."
~ Frederick Buechner

The recurring call tugged at me: *I should check out hospital chaplaincy.* I waited, in part, because of my family. To become a hospital chaplain, one must get a Master of Divinity degree, which meant going back to school for three years and then clinical pastoral education for at least one more year in the hospital.

David wisely reminded me when I was on the fence about pursuing a graduate degree, "Look, those years are gonna fly by anyway, you may as well be working toward something you love."

He didn't know at the time which direction I was headed. I dreaded telling my arty, intellectual, New England family. My journey had been mostly private, and part of my "privacy" was out of fear. Fear of being teased, not only by my family, but other people, even friends. I also had to deal with my own doubts. I wanted to be able to explain what was happening to me, but it was hard to disclose.

At first, I investigated a graduate degree in social work, which made sense and seemed more acceptable, but lacked the spiritual piece I craved. I wanted to connect people with the transcendent, as well as with resources and support, to empower them and let them know they weren't alone. I wanted to delve deeper into the mystery of human suffering and transformation.

So, I quietly applied to Duke Divinity School and when I was accepted, told my mother and David first.

"You're *what*??" mother questioned, in disbelief.

My brother didn't say much, but shrugged, "Hmmm, okay, that's Christian, right?"

With two small children at home, one of whom was still nursing, I enrolled in one class in which to dip my toe. I chose a class called *Prayer*, which was taught by Father Phillip Leach, a priest at the Catholic Newman Center for UNC students. I loved that class. Father Phillip was funny and passionate. He made the Paschal Mystery come alive that Easter, and I hung on his every word.

We read books that fed my soul, like Catherine Doherty's *Molchanie, The Silence of God*. Some students warned me this was *not* like any other classes in the divinity school, and that the program was more like a graduate school for business.

One classmate said, "This is the easiest class you'll take."

Plus, the classes were scheduled between 9-3:00 each day, a time frame that wouldn't work with two small children at home and a husband who was struggling to make ends meet.

So, after completing my prayer class, I pivoted and applied for Duke's training internship for wannabe chaplains at the medical center. I'd test the waters before committing to three years of graduate school. Maybe I'd get this niggling out of my system.

But sitting and listening to patients felt very natural to me and I was relatively comfortable sitting quietly with dead bodies. I found something that gave me purpose. There was life right there amid dying and grief. I was reminded of my dad's death.

As Buddhist Teacher Joan Halifax says, "If you want to learn how to live, spend time with a dying person."

Being affirmed by my supervisors stroked my confidence. "Heidi's a diamond in the rough," one supervisor wrote in my evaluation.

Secretly though, being in the hospital also made me feel connected to my father.

In some ways, the early days of chaplaincy were the most intense. Clinical Pastoral Education (CPE) is an action-reflection-action model of learning and turned out to be a vocational awakening for me. As a chaplaincy student, I got to witness holy encounters and it gave me the learning and scaffolding I needed to serve others. As an intern at Duke, fresh out of the gates, I was learning theories of caregiving the sick and dying, and then practicing them with patients, their families, and staff.

One of the skills CPE students are taught is reflective listening, a special way of being with someone and deeply listening to what they are saying. The chaplain is the only clinician who doesn't ask anything of the patient. What you do instead, is listen intently. You listen for the emotions beneath the surface, below their words. Then you repeat it back to see if you understood. It's a way for the person to feel heard and seen.

And let's face it, that's what we all want most, to be heard and validated. Then you're able to help them sift through their experiences, to try and help them make sense of what is happening.

Penny, my chaplain supervisor, was bubbly, funny, open, and insightful. Our group was her first unsupervised one, as she was training to be a supervisor and educator of chaplain students. Part of our semester-long training was to meet as a group and reflect on our patient visits.

We wrote up patient case studies, which are aptly called verbatims, like a screenplay. We read them aloud and offered and received feedback from each other and Penny. We learned what we did well and places where alternative responses or questions may have made the visit more helpful.

We took a deep dive into our own beliefs as well. We looked closely at the ones we learned growing up, from our parents and religious institutions. Learning about family systems theory (Kerr and Bowen, 1988) was a gamechanger for me. It's a theory of human behavior that defines the family unit as a complex social system, in which members interact to influence each other's behavior. This gave me a new lens from which to view my alcoholic family of origin and helped me to depersonalize the dysfunction.

CPE, as it's called, pushed me to question why I wanted to 'sit on the mourning bench' with people, which Yale Philosophy Professor and Theologian Nicholas Wolterstorff coined so beautifully in his memoir, *Lament for a Son*.

But where I did my real learning was while I was on call, covering the whole hospital as the only in-house chaplain. Chaplains are paged to every death. It's hospital policy, whether the patient or family requests a chaplain or not. Part of this thinking is that we're an extra set of hands, and present as much for staff to alleviate their stress, as the family.

Of the five women in my chaplaincy group, I was continually paged to the most deaths on overnight calls. 'Death Queen' became my nickname, with sometimes as many as eight deaths to attend to in one overnight shift. I began journaling after my on-calls to process my night and what I witnessed. Sometimes a poem would spill out and after my first night working in the hospital this is what came:

### A Prayer for Jacob

A mother's now familiar soft,
wailing lament
that echoes a despairing depth
I know not.
Could You be there hushing and rocking
her in your arms? Is that You reminding
her to breathe, while her babe silently
sleeps swaddled in her arms?
"Cutie pie" followed by kisses from both
on his forehead as natural as if he awoke.
Their surrounding love so pure and beautiful to see.
Honored, teary-eyed, heart-broken – all three,
I know Holy Ground is what this must be.
This prayer is for Jacob, his mom and his Dad,
for Joseph, his brother, who won't understand.
It's for his grandparents too – overwhelmingly sad.
May You be with them now,
help them walk and go on.
And with all other families
who have lost and still long.

My main assignment was the oncology unit, coincidentally where my father had been treated. I even worked with some of the doctors and staff that had been my father's healthcare providers. Part of the chaplain's job is to help a patient who is dying, sift through their memories and their experiences, the good and bad, to glean some meaning and peace before they die.

Surgeon Atul Gawande said so beautifully in his book *Being Mortal*, "If there's anything to be said, in the end, it is just this: the pain of our loss is the greatest evidence we can offer for the importance and meaning of life."

"I want you to pray with me," Danny said soon after his diagnosis of lung cancer was handed down. He had paged me himself and asked to see me right away when he was admitted to the hospital. Even as the new oncology chaplain intern, I knew this was rare for a patient. Usually, we got referrals to see patients from nurses.

"I am not going to just lie here and die," he told me.

"You sound determined," I said trying to stay with him, "I will pray with and for you."

This is how my relationship began with Danny, a man who captivated me during his month-long hospitalization. And although I did not know it then, this formative experience was one that would help confirm the type of work I hoped to do in the future.

Danny was never alone. There was his entourage, which included many members of his motorcycle gang, as well as family members and other close friends. They came in droves, camped out, and catered to him. Danny held court with them, allowing certain friends in his room at times and excusing others when he needed to rest. He even made a sign for his door that read, "Ten-minute time limit on visits."

With his long hair and playboy bunny tattoos, Danny was different than my other patients.

As my supervisor said after a conjoint visit with him, "They seem like a rough crowd."

It's true they did. Black leather jackets and dagger tattoos were the norm and his room often smelled of stale smoke, but in the end these things didn't matter. I was coming to terms with my own grief so I could offer 'hospitality' to all individuals, regardless of their type. The Buddhist Nun, Pema Chodron, taught me to 'know my darkness.' She says the more you know your own, the more space you have for others.

Even so, I did feel intimidated by this crowd's tough exteriors and inside jokes and wondered, *don't they have to get back to work? What is it about Danny that they cannot leave him? And why am I so drawn to him?*

His charm drew people in. Danny had a twinkle in his eye. He knew the power of buying gifts and showered people with them. Early on in his hospitalization, he visited the gift shop and purchased angel paraphernalia for his friends and family, according to their personalities. Some got angel pins, some pens and other little angel statues. He even surprised his nurse, Kathy, who was eight months pregnant, with a rose on Valentine's Day. His extreme politeness and magnetism belied his dagger tattoo on his arm and made him a favorite among the staff.

Danny often had one or two women close by him, slowly brushing his long, dark hair or fiddling with his IV pole, untangling twisted lines. Imagine the lion in the *Wizard of Oz*, flocked by hairdressers and manicurists primping and grooming him. He dismissed these women when I came to visit.

Like Danny, I witnessed my dad's humor, fear, and genuine self as he fought for his life. He got really honest and courageous during his final months. Dying was hard work in more ways than one. When my father couldn't sleep at night because of pain, he wrote letters to his family and friends, thanking them for their friendship and recounting funny stories.

He wanted us to know how much we meant to him and thank us for being a part of his life. "No regrets," he said, "I've had a good life. Take the bad with the good."

Danny never got to the chemotherapy stage. He fought a lung infection his whole stay in the hospital and died before ever starting treatment. But he too, seemed to be working on unfinished business.

Danny vented and confessed and dreamt with me. He disclosed his disconnected relationship with his daughter, Terry, his only child. Danny had been an absentee father most of her life, popping in and out randomly when he was sober.

"I'm turning over a new leaf," he told me.

When he called her to tell her he was sick, he started the conversation by saying, "Terry, I hope you can forgive me. I love you. And I want to make amends."

Danny feared dying but spoke with conviction when he told me he was going to beat his cancer, and since he had already won a battle against Hodgkin's Disease as a teenager, I didn't put it past him. He had a new goal of becoming "a preacher," if God would help him heal just one more time.

"There's a reason why He spared me the first time," Danny told me.

As difficult as that time was on the cancer unit with my father, I found something real and meaningful. I was witnessing it again as I accompanied Danny. Although we were from different worlds, there was a common thread. Grief is universal after all, the most human of our experiences.

As Penelope Wilcock says in her wonderful passage in, *Spiritual Care of Dying and Bereaved People*, "The sacred territory of death is a place which asks questions of us (too). Is it hard for me to be honest? Is it frightening to find myself in a situation of physical, spiritual and emotional intimacy with someone? How do I feel about deep helplessness—the moments when I can do nothing, say nothing, only be with you? Or would I rather walk away from that? When you confront me with your confusion, and your grief, can I look at that steadily? Or do I take refuge in evasions and lies?"[1]

---

[1]    Penelope Wilcock, Spiritual Care of Dying and bereaved People, (Society for Promoting Christian Knowledge, 1996), p. 2.

I had always longed for my father to tell me he loved me. On the occasions when he did, he had usually been drinking, so I discounted it. However, in my father's last letter to me, he ended it, "With only the love a father can give." It was his final gift to me.

Danny gave me gifts that I have carried with me as well. He knew what he needed and was direct about it. He paged me and asked for me several times during his hospitalization, which pushed me to show up and be present no matter what his situation was.

"I'm scared," he said when he was transferred to the intensive care unit for his worsened infection. "If I go to sleep, I may not wake up. Will you pray with me?"

Like his many devoted friends and family, Danny reached me in a way that reeled me in and held my attention. Although I wondered about it at the time, I now know it is what the Dalai Lama calls identification compassion. This is the compassion one feels when you have suffered in a particular way and then feel strongly about alleviating the suffering for others who experience the same loss.

As a caregiver, I wanted Danny and his family to have the same experience my father and family had. So, when he could no longer breathe on his own and had to be intubated, I felt incredibly disappointed.

Danny reminded me of Jesus with his long hair and crowds of people around him all the time. His girlfriend, and his oldest friend Christine, seemed to rotate the Martha and Mary roles from the Bible, sometimes fixing things in the room, and other times just weeping and sitting with him. His other friend, John, and his brother, Tony, reminded me of disciples the way they spoke of him, especially after intubation when he couldn't speak.

Danny had his people around him all the time, the familiar faces and always new visitors. I like to think Danny found in our visits the solace Jesus found leaving the crowds and retreating to a mountain or lake. He repented his "evil ways" of drugs and adultery to me and asked for forgiveness.

I didn't know the specifics of his past, but when he was transferred to the intensive care unit and scores of weeping people followed him, I understood when his nurse said, "It's not like he's been an angel or anything."

Years later, when I bounced this insight off my priest friend, Liz, she shared an image from the medieval monk, Brother Lawrence. He sees all of us as trees in winter, with little to give, stripped of leaves and color and growth, whom God loves unconditionally anyway.

I tried to be an anchor in the midst of a big, unfamiliar hospital during a very scary, unsafe time. A non-anxious, friendly presence who'd accompany Danny, and my other patients, through the stressful medical environment. It's a miracle that Danny made it off the intensive care unit when the doctor extubated him because he was expected to rapidly decline and die within an hour. But when doctors give someone a limited time to live, they aren't always right.

My father made it only four days from when we left the hospital the last time, even though his doctor estimated two weeks. Danny on the other hand, not only made it back to the oncology floor, but also spoke and joked with his friends that evening. He paged me that night and was disappointed when the on-call chaplain arrived.

He wanted me to see him "off the vent", which is short for a ventilator, a tube placed down his throat and breathing for him. I wanted to as well and was surprised when I got to his room the next day because Danny was agonally breathing, the belabored and ceasing of breathing associated with the moments before death.

Danny resembled the frightened person in Edward Munch's, *The Scream*, with his hollowed face and fearful gaze. He was hanging on by sucking inhalations that were spaced further and further apart. He looked disheveled and all the color was drained from his pale, almost gray face. Beads of sweat formed on his brow and along his long lion's mane hair. It was pulled back off his face revealing its gauntness and his unfocused eyes were open although partially covered by an oxygen mask.

Danny was weak and limp and a well-worn sheet barely covered his emaciated, fragile frame. His mother, brother, daughter Terry, and best friend Christine were sitting uncomfortably in the room watching him.

Remembering my own father's guttural and intentional last breaths, I thought it would be a matter of moments before Danny died, but after thirty minutes or so, I recalled that agonal breathing could go on for hours. I worried about not having time to visit my other patients but knew I would stay with Danny.

His nurse, Tom, popped his head in and said, "If y'all need anything let me know," and turned around and walked out of the room.

I was a bit surprised that this was the extent of help Danny's family was being offered while he lay dying. I felt they deserved more guidance during this intense and major transitional time and so we prayed, gently rubbed his feet, spoke with him and put his Bible under his hand. Looking back, I know now that the nurse, Tom, simply didn't know what to do to help Danny and his family. He was stuck in his own anxiety and grief.

As Danny persisted, I got the feeling he was waiting for something, too. We told him he could "go" and that it was okay. Terry told him she loved him. We thanked him for his many gifts and strength, but he still suffered on, painfully fighting off death.

My father's final death scene seemed more peaceful than this. He was in a familiar and comfortable place. Like Danny, his family surrounded him, but he also had Mr. K, his favorite cat, curled up on the end of his bed. He had his dignity. That is what was missing here.

I remembered it was also what my father had feared losing the most. "I just don't want to lose my dignity."

So, when I opened my eyes and saw the twisted, partially soiled sheet barely covering Danny's genitals, I thought about what Danny would want. He would want his dignity, too. What would this look like to him in the context of this sterile hospital environment and what "comforts from his home" could I recreate?

I remembered that he liked his long hair brushed down in front of his shoulders. And his friend Christine had shared with me how particular he was about his clothes as well, especially his T-shirts.

"It has to be the perfect one and the right color," she revealed. "One time before he was diagnosed and after a bout of throwing up, he refused to wear the clean shirt I got for him. He is very picky."

"Is that a Carolina Panthers T-shirt?" He asked leaning over the toilet bowl.

"What difference does it make?" Christine replied in disbelief.

"It matters," he shot back. "I am not going to wear that black Panther's shirt. Get my blue Earnhardt one."

I suggested we change his sweaty, wrinkled, falling-off gown and we worked from there. I shared the plan with his family and two best friends who were present in the room. We sprang into action to give our final gifts of dignity and peace to Danny.

I alerted the nurse that we wanted to change his sheets, give him a bath and change him into a clean gown. Once the nurse sensed what was happening, he practically ran to get a pail and washcloths and it was then that I realized he just hadn't known what to do for them.

Everyone was quietly focused. I explained the biblical significance of cleansing Danny's body, "washing his feet and anointing him with oil." This was done to Jesus before His death and that similarly, it was a way of honoring Danny and preparing him for the dignified death he would want. I pulled the curtain and left the family to bathe him.

As I waited outside the room, his two nurses spoke with me and seemed less evasive. They changed his sheets, the tape on his arms holding his IV lines in place and cleared out old glasses and clutter in the room. Finally, his brother, Tony, came out and asked me if it was possible for me to baptize Danny.

*Why didn't I think of that?* That's what Danny was waiting for. He might have been too embarrassed to ask me when he could still speak. I agreed and gathered what I needed while they finished washing him. I quickly got some sterilized water and ran to the pediatric floor for a couple of seashells from which to pour the water, while mentally planning a brief service.

*Now this looks like Danny* I thought, when I came back in the room. I couldn't believe this was the same dying man. His hair was clean and brushed perfectly down either side of his face, falling below his bony shoulders.

All the sweat and gunk around his eyes and forehead had been cleaned off, which almost gave a shine to his face. His dry, cracked lips looked smoother and less painful. He wore a clean, baby-blue gown and was covered with new, crisp sheets. The room smelled better and looked cleaner and felt less claustrophobic with the curtains opened and pulled to the side.

"His gown even matches his oxygen mask," Christine pointed out proudly.

"You look great," I said to Danny noticing longer spaces between his breaths, "I am going to baptize you now."

In some denominations, like the United Church of Christ, chaplain students have permission to baptize people in an "emergency" situation, like in the hospital. This was my first. We all gathered around his bed with Christine standing at his head, stroking his hair while tears streamed down her cheeks. Everybody bowed heads and after a brief service from my borrowed pocket edition *Book of Worship,* I dripped the water from the seashell onto his head and baptized him in the name of the Father, and of the Son, and of the Holy Spirit.

The phone rang then, and it was one of Danny's ex-girlfriends demanding to speak with him. As Tony hung up on her, I knew this was a perfect ending for Danny, being the center of attention with women still fighting over him. As soon as I said, "Amen" at the end of a final prayer, Danny lowered his head onto his left shoulder toward Christine and released his last breath.

Loud shrieks came from his brother. He hugged Tom, the young nurse. They had connected in a way only a few know from traveling together through this rite of passage. It turns out this was Tom's first patient death, and he shared a little about his grandfather's recent passing while gently removing Danny's oxygen mask.

After he took off the mask, I could really see Danny's face and I concentrated intently on it as if searching for something. His eyes were still half-open and although I tried to close his eyelids, they seemed stuck. When I stared into them, I saw Jesus again, and this time it was the suffering one, the wounded Jesus who empathizes with our deepest pain.

But I kept looking. Much later I realized I was searching for my father.

It was as if I was waiting to see if I would meet him there, silently asking, "Is that you, Dad? Are you there?"

Each time I was paged to a death there was a part of me half expecting to see the face I saw during my first death. As I peeked around the curtain and saw the still, silent body, whose whole history was a mystery to me, I was also looking for a glimpse of my father.

By baptizing Danny and preparing him for death, by "washing his feet and anointing him with oil," we hallowed him, mindful of his dignity, and surrounded him with love and peace. Creating a space of comfort, even in a cold, sterile environment, is important for a person who is leaving this world and for their family who are present. You honor them and promote healthier grieving for the loved ones left behind.

I gave the seashells to each of Danny's best friends and as they placed them in his relaxed fist, they told me they would bury them with him, along with his Bible.

Caring for Danny struck a deep place in me and affirmed the importance of working with dying people, their families, and the hospital staff who care for them. It is a holy space. Hospital caregivers need to be well-supported and encouraged to process their own experiences to stay balanced. The more present caregivers can be during this time, the more closure the dying patient and family will have.

Terry was there while her father was dying, and Danny knew it. Something changed in him when he saw her, he was calmer, as if he dropped below the fear and pain. At the end of life, some of the grudges we hold seem silly.

My father waited for my younger brother, Scott, to get home from graduate school in Austin before he died. He wanted to lay eyes on him and tell him he loved him. They'd had a tempestuous relationship and Dad wanted to say good-bye.

Scott was the "absent-minded professor" of our family. My great-grandmother Gracie called him a human walkie-talkie as he would always chatter away as a child. I passed my history classes in school because of Scott. He explained the Korean War to me and why the U.S. had no business in Vietnam. His favorite movie was the *The Bridge on the River Kwai*, one I could never quite get through.

Scott was smart and got perfect scores on standardized tests. Whereas my father and older brother, David, liked competitive sports like football and basketball, Scott preferred sailing. My father had little patience with him at times, leaving my mother feeling a need to intervene and defend him.

But my dying father waited for him, nonetheless. Forgiveness can be hard. It requires at least one party getting vulnerable and uneasy. But resolving unfinished business is an important piece of work for all of us at the end of life.

Death turns out to be a great equalizer. It doesn't matter if you are rich or poor, Democrat or Republican, black, or white, religious or not so much. Sooner or later, death's going to come knocking on your door. Dying people teach you to pay attention and to forgive and to not sweat the small stuff.

## REFLECTION QUESTIONS

I invite you to use the following prompts for reflection, journaling, or conversation:

- When have you felt "deep helplessness" with someone, not able to do anything but just be with them?

- Who in your life actively listens to you and makes you feel heard? What is it that makes you feel 'seen'?

- When have you ever felt a connection with someone who's experienced a similar loss as you? What was that like?

- What are your takeaways from Danny's story?

# 8

## SEEDS OF NEW BEGINNINGS

"When I dare to be powerful – to use my strength
in the service of my vision, then it becomes
less and less important whether I am afraid."
~ Audre Lorde

"Whoo cooks for you, whoo cooks for you all?" In the wee hours of the night a questioning owl hooted outside my bedroom window, and in the darkness, Matt reminded me about this great bird's lament.

I'm by no means a night owl, but in chaplain school you often pull all-nighters while on-call, caring for people. You have to. It's part of your training. And when answering a call, you do things you never thought you'd do.

I knew somewhere deep down in my soul, since my father's death, that I was called to work with people near the end of life. During a crisis, as a "non-anxious presence," as it's called, I was able to walk with people, accompany them during the scariest and most difficult times of their lives.

A common lament among end-of-life patients and their families was, "This is the hardest thing I will ever do."

What a tremendous honor to offer hospitality and support during such an intimate time. One night I sat with a distraught mother in the hospital room of her son who had a cardiac arrest and died in his ICU bed.

"This wasn't supposed to happen," Shawn's mother, Arnetta wept. "He's supposed to sing and inspire people. I just thought … because of that, he would make it." I could only shrug and shake my head.

Shawn was a twenty-six-year-old black man from the South, studying to be an opera singer in London, at the Royal College. One year earlier, he'd been diagnosed with cardiomyopathy, a chronic disorder affecting the muscle of his heart. He'd been in and out of hospitals ever since, always hoping to get it under control so he could get back to his passion of singing.

His clothes were still hanging in his dormitory room in London and Arnetta worried about how she'd get them home. If you can believe it, his younger brother, Sammy, had died of the same condition the previous year.

Arnetta and I spent most of the night together in silence while Shawn's large body lay still on the bed next to us. While she quietly wept, I thought, *This is humanity at its most raw and naked. Sitting in a room with your dead child.*

The grace is that in that vulnerable, mysterious place, it seemed as though God was there too. In those quiet moments, the Presence was palpable. The hours we spent together felt sacred, as if we were in a liminal space, connected in another dimension of time.

Episcopalian Bishop Katherine Jefferts Schori said, "God does not cause suffering or punish people with it, but God is present and known more intimately in the midst of suffering."

This was certainly my experience, and of all my families, Arnetta was the clearest example I ever witnessed of the reality of God's presence in suffering. That doesn't fix the suffering or stop it, but it did give her a companion whose compassionate presence somehow buoyed her to be able to endure what she was experiencing.

As I drove away from the hospital the next morning, the sun shone brightly as it climbed into the sky, as if nothing had happened. I turned on the radio and happened to catch then end of Great Sacred Music on WCPE, our local public radio station. A bass voice bellowed *O Isis Und Osiris* from Mozart's opera, 'The Magic Flute' and my eyes filled with tears. As often happens in the hospital, I never saw Arnetta again, and to this day, think of her and Shawn whenever I hear opera music.

Shortly after my chaplain internship, I started a year-long clinical pastoral education residency program at UNC Hospitals and continued learning and discerning my passion. CPE taught me, in the words of theologian John Karl, "to construct hospitable places, sanctuaries, and to hear the voice of marginalized stories." We can be places of grace for one another and know firsthand the value of support, especially in the midst of grief.

One night while on call, I realized a real need in the hospital. As I was walking parents, who were obviously in shock, out to the main doors of the hospital after their young adult son had died from injuries in a motor vehicle crash, I heard myself say, "Well, take care, good luck to you."

Once the doors closed and they were safely gone, I rolled my eyes, shook my head, and thought, *we can do better than this.* There was no formalized bereavement care in place for adults. When families headed to the parking garage, leaving their loved ones for the final time, that was the last support they received from the hospital.

This bothered me. I wanted to support grieving families and help them adjust to their new norm. In a supervision meeting, I floated the idea of a follow-up service to my supervisor.

"Trust your intuition," she encouraged.

So, with the help of my supervisor and our pastoral care department director, we formed a hospital-wide, interdisciplinary bereavement advisory council to develop and create the hospital's first adult bereavement program, with the goal of attending to the emotional pain that results from loss and death. Our mission: "To provide inclusive, collaborative and comprehensive bereavement care, support, resources, and education to patients, families, staff, and the community."

The UNC Hospitals Bereavement Support Service was born shortly after my residency, in 2002, and I was hired 15 hours a week to manage it. One of my most important responsibilities was making sure family members received grief materials. So, let's say you had an adult loved one die in the hospital. Since it's a policy to page the chaplain at the time of death, if you were present, the chaplain would give you a packet of grief information and resources right then. If you weren't there, the packet would be mailed to you by the chaplain of that unit. It was a good reminder that "you are not alone."

Inside the packet there's also a condolence letter, followed in six months by a card and six months later, by an anniversary card. This way, if you stumbled out of the hospital dazed and confused after your beloved family member died, there'd be notes and grief resources coming your way throughout the year ahead.

I would've loved that.

Think about how you would feel if you received cards from the hospital where your husband or wife, father, mother, or fill in the blank, died, letting you know you were on their minds during this difficult time. I often received cards or phone calls from people thanking UNC Hospitals. "I can't believe you remembered my dear James and me. Imagine my surprise when I walked to the mailbox and saw your note. It means so much to me to know you're still there."

Helping navigate the many changes following the death of a significant loved one promotes better adapting and healthier grieving. Receiving information about the nature of grief and its likely course can help normalize what's happening which may increase a sense of control. Plus, knowing support is available can be comforting.

The bereavement program created good continuity of care for families from the hospital as well. From the administration's point of view, the UNC Bereavement Support Service created value for the hospital by extending the optimal care of their patients to include their families.

This was all great and fine, except for the fact that my second marriage was falling apart. Matt and I were growing apart and things were getting harder at home. He had a rapidly increasing interest in organic farming and grass-fed beef. I was caring for dying and grieving people and moving further into the world of chaplaincy. Oh, and tennis.

Let me explain. As an employee of the hospital, I was eligible to join the university's swim and tennis club called, *The Farm*. This was perfect, since the kids could take tennis and swim lessons there and attend camp during the summers. Check off the childcare box.

Plus, we'd have a cool place to hang out during the sweltering summer months. Now I must admit to you there was some nostalgia for me in joining *The Farm*. I grew up going to clubs, swimming, and playing tennis with friends and my family. This would be a pleasant link to my past.

I realize I'm going out on a limb here confessing this. Many people didn't grow up with these luxuries and I'm aware of how incredibly fortunate I was to have these havens to escape to. It wasn't until I was older that I understood their more superficial aspects, as well.

Still, some of my happiest memories are from spending time at Tatnuck Country Club, doing flips off the diving board and drying off in the sun by lying on the hot cement. I remember the first time I nervously swam the length of the pool, allowing me the freedom to be in the deep end by myself. You may remember this rite of passage for yourself, or a different one from your childhood that is equally important. Either way, the point is, having fond summer memories.

But Matt wasn't interested in *The Farm*. He didn't like pools and didn't play tennis, although I tried to get him interested. He was a good athlete and played baseball in high school, so I thought it was worth a shot. I signed us up for a mixed doubles event that involved playing a tennis round-robin with several couples, followed by a cookout on the deck. *What a great way to get out and do something fun together and meet new people,* I thought. But Matt showed zero interest and didn't want to do it.

Nonetheless, getting back into tennis turned out to be a great outlet, both physically and socially. I loved the sport and grew up playing year-round, indoors in the winter months, of course. I'd gotten away from it in college, but as they say, after 20 years without lifting a racquet, it was just like riding a bike.

Working all week in the hospital and grinding it out in graduate school made whacking the ball around with new friends something to look forward to. It was physically satisfying as well, and I didn't think about anything while running around the court. This helped me forget about my failing marriage.

I must've been playing a *lot* of tennis. One day Matt mused, "I wish there was a way for you to make money playing tennis."

Noah started to get into tennis, too, taking semi-private lessons after school.

Addie was more into diving, and was really good at it. The diving coach pulled me aside one day, saying, "Addie has real potential, and if she got serious about it, could probably dive in college if she wanted."

Meanwhile, Matt started work as an extension officer for the county and wanted us to move out into the country onto a communal farm. Clearly, Matt and I weren't going to make it for the long haul.

My sister-in-law, Nina, suggested marriage therapy. "Then you'll know you tried everything and left no stone unturned."

We tried therapy but it didn't last long. Our counselor was brutally honest: "You want different things in life, and I just don't see you staying together."

Basically, we got fired from marriage therapy. "Who's in charge of getting the bills paid?" Matt and I just looked at each other blankly. "Well, Noah and Addie aren't going to do it," he rebuked.

Right then and there I knew I needed to take responsibility for the care of our children and make sure everything they needed was tended to.

Soon after, we separated. I hated that. But it did confirm what I knew to be true in my heart.

I also needed to go back and finish divinity school if I wanted to be an ordained minister to become a certified, professional chaplain and continue to manage the bereavement program. With a colleague's suggestions and help, I applied to, was accepted by, and transferred my credits from Duke Divinity School, to a smaller, less prestigious, Baptist one.

It's not where I would've gone if I had my druthers, but the program was structured with second-career, working adults in mind. The schedules worked well with my newly single-parenting lifestyle and work responsibilities. I could take mostly evening classes and attend day classes only a couple times a week. This allowed me to be home for my school-aged children, as well as work part-time as the bereavement chaplain at the hospital.

I completed the three-year Master of Divinity degree in four years. The biggest surprise was how wonderful my time at Campbell Divinity School was! As the "token liberal," from the day I interviewed, I felt accepted, supported, and loved.

Plus, the one-hour drive there and back, was mostly along a tree-lined lake that featured blue herons, beautiful sunrises and sunsets, and gave me some much-needed solitude. When I graduated in 2007, I was ordained as a United Church of Christ Minister with a full-time 'call' to clinical chaplaincy at UNC Hospitals.

## REFLECTION QUESTIONS

I invite you to use the following prompts for reflection, journaling, or conversation:

- When have you experienced God's presence in the midst of suffering?
- Where is a special place for you from your childhood? What made it significant?
- What have you brought into the world that without you wouldn't exist?
- When have you been surprised by a place or people you had pre-conceived notions about?

# 9

## GRIEF GROUP

"Never underestimate the power of a small
group of committed people to change the world.
In fact, it is the only thing that ever has."
~Margaret Mead

"Plunge into matter. Plunge into God.
By means of all created things, without exception, the
divine assails us, penetrates us and molds us.
We imagine it as distant
and inaccessible, whereas in fact,
we live steeped in its burning layers."
~Pierre Teilhard de Chardin

"A spiritual person tries less to be
godly than to be deeply human.
~William Sloane Coffin

A large part of the bereavement service was a grief
recovery group, open to families and friends who lost
loved ones in the hospital or community. We created
a safe space for people to gather and share their stories. Social
support facilitates healthy grieving because you spend time
with other people who "get it." Trust me, no one ever wants

to have to join this group, but it can reduce the isolation and loneliness that often accompanies grief.

I co-facilitated grief recovery groups on Monday evenings for 15 years with my chaplain and grief counselor colleague, Darryl. An end-of-life student chaplain mentee attended these sessions each year, too, training to facilitate groups and "hold space" for the groups.

I can't say I ever really looked forward to the groups on Monday evenings but kept offering them for reasons I can't quite understand. Still, the moment I walked in and saw the brave faces gathered with the hope of some relief, we'd start talking, and before you knew it, we were wrapping up for the night.

You know how that is, when you have a meeting or class in the evening and all day you carry it around with you with a sort of foreboding? You pray there'll be a small hurricane or maybe a blizzard and it'll be canceled. Or perhaps no one will show up.

But when the time comes, it's lovely. You connect and feel energized and grateful that you get to spend time with these beautiful human beings who are courageously bearing witness to each other. Spiritual teacher Ram Dass makes an excellent point, "We're all just walking each other home."

At 89 years old, Betty joined one of our eight-week grief-group sessions. Her granddaughter drove her every Monday evening and she never missed a meeting. Betty came to the group because of a recurring dream she'd had for more than 50 years!

Every night she dreamt of her first husband, a fighter pilot in World War II, who was shot down and killed in combat. She replayed the moment when the military police came to the door, knocked, and told her that her husband was dead. Betty was playing bridge at the time with other military wives and pregnant with their first child, a girl. She remembers the billowy blue dress she was wearing that expanded with her growing belly.

Betty joined the group to try and work through her recurring dream and the traumatic death of her first husband, so she would feel some peace before she died. She was very clear about her intention.

Betty had remarried and had a son with her second husband. She shared he was "a fine man," and raised her daughter as his own. Having never met her own father, her daughter knew of no other and loved and protected her stepdad. I got the feeling that Betty's first husband was the love of her life, but she was also grateful to have met a good man and have a second successful marriage. They had a long, happy marriage until he died of cancer years later.

Betty's dreams persisted, however. And slowly, by sharing her traumatic story of loss, and by listening to others, Betty happily reported at the end of our time together, that her recurring dream stopped! It no longer plagued her, and she could live the rest of her life freely and die a peaceful woman. There's power in bearing witness to each other in groups, and Betty was astonished that by connecting with others around loss, healing could happen for her.

Every death, especially traumatic ones, change your life forever. With a traumatic loss, an extra step is necessary in the grieving process. One must process the actual death itself before moving through "normal" mourning stages. For Betty, hearing about her husband's plane crash — the sights, sounds, smells, the event itself, needed processing before she could grieve her life without him.

When the group ended, I didn't hear from Betty again, but I did hear from our hospital president. She wrote him a beautiful multi-paged letter describing her experience, about how helpful and healing the group was for her.

Grief is hard work. Integrating grief into a meaningful future does not come automatically or easily. It is a long-term process, not a "quick fix." But if you can muster the courage to speak your mind with your heart and tell your story, sharing can cut your grief in half and double your joy.

Betty's openness and vulnerability to share her lingering heartache created an opportunity for the group to listen and share in her pain. Her groupmates "listened her into being" and into wholeness.

Plus, the weekly presentations offered useful information on grief's journey. We shared education about different aspects of grief, including anticipatory mourning, (the grief you feel before a death), coping, getting through holidays, and the myriad of emotions that arise. "I think I'm going crazy," was a common refrain.

I could totally relate to this from my father's death. "I know what you mean," I said, sharing my experience of wanting to roll down the window at stoplights and yell at people for not caring.

One of the most popular topics was, *Who Am I Now? Grief and Loss as an Identity Crisis.* You feel unmoored after someone you love dies. How are you supposed to know who you are when they're gone? "Taking care of my husband was my job for 18 months," one widow shared. "I'm not sure what to do with myself now."

It's scary to walk into a grief group the first time (and second, and maybe third). One member shared, "I must admit I almost turned around and walked out the first day. At the end when we were prompted to think of 'three things you're grateful for,' one of my answers was that I stayed in the room!"

We closed each session with a poem. My co-facilitator Darryl always reminded, "Do something you enjoy when you get home. You've done a lot of work this evening — watch a comedy or sports on TV, play with your pet, perhaps take a bath. Have a glass of wine. Something for YOU."

Years later I learned the term that describes what was unfolding in me from the Celtic world. "Ex-centration" is "finding your true self outside of yourself or finding your true center in the heart of one another and at the heart of all life." In other words, I was finding a new framework for my life, something bigger than me and my family, by losing myself in what I loved, not driven by my ego, but from my true self, made by God.

"Ex-centration" was coined by the French Jesuit priest, scientist, and mystic, Pierre Teilhard de Jardin. Born in May, 1881, Teilhard was a man ahead of his time. He believed and wrote about the sacredness of the universe, seeing the sacred in art and the earth. He said ex-centration or service, is "heaven on earth."

Teilhard had a traditional French Catholic religious upbringing and was raised to believe the dualism of Western thought — namely that spirit and matter were separate entities. But Teilhard believed all matter is sacred and that at the heart of matter, is the heart of God. He describes being drawn to matter from an early age, and more specifically describes, "by something that shone at the heart of matter."

Teilhard worried about his belief and that he might be a pantheist, but in a dream, he heard the words from St. Matthew's Gospel, in Latin, *Ego sum, noli timere* ("It is I; do not be afraid" 14:27). Teilhard heard these words not from afar but whispered deeply within himself. The assurance that came to him in that moment was: "Do not be afraid to see matter as sacred; do not be afraid to adore this Light that is deep in all things. It is I."

Reading about this sounded similar to the moment in my Honda.

During World War I, Teilhard was a stretcher-bearer in the French army. He experienced the Presence again, in the midst of the horror of war. It was here that Teilhard experienced the suffering presence of Love. It is here that he invites us to look for the Presence, as well as the infinite beauty and wildness of creation and the limitless imagination and longings of the human spirit. Teilhard wrote after horrendous battles, "More than ever, I believe that life is beautiful."

Of course, the church didn't like Teilhard's teachings and silenced him. The Vatican banned his theological writings, and he was forbidden to teach, or even discuss his ideas. The church exiled him to America.

It was in America that Teilhard began to talk about "sacrifice of service" and his own ex-centration. Teilhard's love of the world was inseparable from his awareness of the world's sufferings. The heart of the divine could be sought everywhere, in both the glory and the pain of the world.

Teilhard's whimsical way of seeing the world was infectious. My favorite story of his is from *Walking the Dog with Teilhard* by psychologist Jean Houston, who met him in Central Park when she was 14 years old. She tells how "Mr. Tayer," as she called him, went for weekly walks with her and taught about wonder and awe over the simplest things.

"Look, Jean! A rock! A butterfly!" He was astonished by everything. "Jean, look at the caterpillar. Ahhh!" He exclaimed down on his knees. "How beautiful it is… his little green feet on the road to metamorphosis. Jean, can you feel yourself to be a caterpillar?"

"Oh yes," she replied.

"Think of your metamorphosis," he said. "What is the butterfly of Jean?"

Houston says being with Mr. "Tayer" was like "being in attendance of God's own party, a continuous celebration, and its mysteries ... Everything was related to everything else and was very, very good."

Can I tell you how much I love this story? Discovering Teilhard and reading this felt like fresh air for my soul and like an energetic stamp of approval. Here was this person I totally resonated with, and right then and there, Mr. "Tayer" became one of my saints.

Teilhard affirmed what was happening on my path, as well, even down to hearing Divine words from within during a horrible time. Since my mystical visitation, I knew God wasn't contained inside a church, or temple, or mosque, and here was proof. Again. Feeling the Presence in nature, the feathers, and birds, and synchronicities, as well as with my dying father, and people in the hospital and grief groups ... God is there in all of life rooting for me and rooting for you.

As Saint Hildegard of Bingen, the 12th-century Christian mystic so eloquently said, "We need to fly with two wings of awareness. The one wing is an awareness of life's kindness, beauty, and blessedness. The other is an awareness of life's pain, struggle, and suffering. If we try to fly with only one of these, we will be like an eagle trying to fly with only one wing."

In other words, we will not truly see. Teilhard teaches us to love our universe and everything in it in the midst of all of it because there is where you will find God. His teachings, 100 years later, are still prevalent, and arguably needed more today than ever.

Teilhard de Jardin's prayer is,

> "I love you ... Lord Jesus ... you who are as gentle as the human heart, as fiery as the forces of nature, as intimate as life itself ... I love you as a world, as *this* world which has captivated my heart."

## REFLECTION QUESTIONS

I invite you to use the following prompts for reflection, journaling, or conversation:

- Do you presently or have you ever had a recurring dream? If so, what meaning does it have for you?

- Have you ever belonged to a small group that allowed you to authentically share your story, bearing witness to one another? What was it that allowed you to feel comfortable in that space?

- Have you experienced "ex-centration," losing yourself in love for something or one another only to truly find yourself? If so, what was it?

- If you took a walk with "Mr. Tayer," I wonder what he might say to you? What would you want him to know about your life?

- Inventor Buckminster Fuller said, "There's nothing in a caterpillar that tells you it's going to be a butterfly." Meditate on Teilhard's butterfly image – like things you'd love to have as part of your future – things that may resemble caterpillars in the early going.

- What is the butterfly of *you*?

# 10

## VORTEX OF AWAKENING

"The wound is the place where the light enters you."
~Rumi

"What if imagination and art are not frosting at all,
but the fountainhead of human experience?"
~Rollo May

My friend with cystic fibrosis taught me about loving-kindness meditations. Tiffany is a beautiful woman who was born with this debilitating disease that damages your lungs, digestive tract, and other organs. CF, as it's known, affects the cells that produce mucus, sweat, and digestive juices.

When Tiffany was born, her parents were told she wouldn't live past eight years old. But in her late thirties she reached out to me at the hospital about working together. Tiffany is a survivor of two double-lung transplants and so grateful to be alive that her life's work, her service to the world, is advocating for hospitalized patients.

I liked Tiffany — smart and spunky — and we hit it off right away. "I've spent most of my life in this hospital, and know the patient perspective, what is helpful, what's not, and believe I'm the one who can share this important information with health-care providers."

There is an incredible story about how Tiffany got her new lungs. First, she was on the donor waiting list forever. Then one day she got a call that there were lungs available for her.

After many tests and lots of preparation, Tiffany bravely went underwent surgery for her new set of lungs. Lying in her hospital bed, after her operation was over, every orifice of her ravaged body was plugged into a machine. She couldn't move or speak, since she had a tube down her throat breathing for her.

Yet Tiffany felt grateful to be alive and passed the time by thinking of positive affirmations and then with her mind, sending them out into the universe. "Thank you for my life … for breath … may I be healthy and whole … may all people be healthy and whole … thank you for my new lungs … thank you for my donor and donor family."

Think of lying immobilized in a hospital bed, totally dependent on others and hooked up to a breathing machine. Maybe you'd be sending out messages of gratitude, but I imagine myself immobilized and scared to death.

But Tiffany wasn't helpless. She dropped beneath the fear and anxiety and tapped into a deeper part of herself, the wise and primordial part that hungered for expression. Connecting with this *chi*, Chinese for vital life-force, she was able to use the power of her mind to send out love and appreciation into the world from her intensive-care hospital bed. Tiffany is a modern-day Teilhard, using her mind to create matter.

Sometimes we're on a spiritual journey without even knowing it. There's a part of us that knows things. A sacred part that wants to find resonance and contribute to the world. Why not connect with this ancient source the next time a challenging situation presents itself? We all have access to this equipoise, this knowing with our head and heart.

Tiffany also affirmed what I was experiencing with my father. Clearly, there is a part of us, our spirit, that lives on after death. For instance, after Tiffany left the hospital, initially she felt okay, but her body started rejecting her lungs. She started developing strange symptoms, too, like craving Doritos! These tortilla chips are something she'd never been a fan of before her transplant.

Tiffany started to feel ill, as her body was rejecting her new lungs, and began shutting down. Her donor was young when she died in a car accident, and Tiffany believes she may have been angry, jealous of her getting to live, and so her lungs weren't settling.

Tiffany was lucky enough to receive a second set of lungs, and this time the transplant was successful. She instantly felt better and instinctively knew her donor was supporting and helping her thrive. And she no longer craved Doritos!

I was in awe of how Tiffany used her active imagination to visualize healthy lungs and her body completely healing, while sending out affirmations to the world. The oldest person I've ever heard of living with cystic fibrosis, at 49 years old, Tiffany manages her own successful patient advocacy business, her service to the world. What a role model for us all.

I told my spiritual director, Karen, about Tiffany's strength, courage, and desire to help others in the midst of her CF diagnosis. "What makes people like Tiffany so freaking fearless?" I asked her. She just looked at me and smiled.

Karen told me about a local Celtic spirituality retreat with John Phillip Newell, a Church of Scotland Minister, author, and teacher of the Celtic tradition. I attended the retreat and saw how Celtic spirituality tied together the disparate pieces I was learning. For example, John reminded us to listen to the "utterances of God" and watch for "thin places," where the line between this material world and the sacred is so thin, it is almost indistinguishable.

The Celtic tradition is one path to awareness that can be traced back centuries and yet is still evolving. The emphasis is on the sacred essence in all living things, including nature. This reminded me of Teilhard's teachings and felt familiar.

Newell teaches that this stream of wisdom wants you to know the holiness of your deepest energies and allow your life to be transformed in the midst of it. In fact, this tradition believes that everything is sacred, including your soul. "Every life-form has a divine spark within," he teaches.

John had a mystical experience of Presence in his early teens. In the middle of the night, he was awakened and aware of the presence of Christ, seated in a chair directly next to his bed. While Christ didn't speak to him, the way he leaned in and paid total attention was powerful and reassuring. Newell's experience was that "Christ was looking into the heart of my being, with love."

Newell kept this experience hidden for nearly 35 years because he didn't know how to speak about it. Only after realizing how many countless other people experienced the Presence, he realized the importance of sharing his. For as he stresses in *Christ of the Celts*, "The experience is one of Love. It is vitally important that we hear from one another so that our fragments of vision, which in isolation can seem strange, together might become a fuller picture of the deeply personal nature of the universe."

Celtic fairy tale author George MacDonald uses the image of a grandmother swaying in her rocking chair up in the attic of a house as a metaphor for the divine within each of us. In his children's book *The Princess and the Goblin*, the grandmother says to the princess, who she's been waiting for, "Come in my dear, come in. I am glad to see you. You are welcome here. This is your home."

You, too, can experience this welcoming, kind grandmother within you.

Celtic spirituality had everything I loved and was already practicing. I was grateful to find a tradition that resonated with me — encouraging love of nature, contemplation, creativity, and active imagination. It's as if, yet again, I was awakened from a dormant slumber and I re-membered parts of myself I'd forgotten, especially creative parts. In the Celtic world, Jesus is seen as lifting the veil to show you what you have forgotten, the most intimate of truths.

I didn't know what I was doing or what it was called at the time, but when I was young and my parents fought in their bedroom, I'd escape in my mind and imagine I was somewhere else, a safer place. I was manifesting for myself an inner spiritual home, a safe haven. Celtic spirituality reminds you that your creative imagination is an essential part of who you are and can be tapped.

Imagination can be your greatest asset if you value and nurture it. This requires some daydreaming, playfulness, and light-heartedness. Let your imagination guide you to new ways of seeing and being in the world.

The resources you need are all around you, so take the mundane and make it magical. I imagined healing arts — creative practices that promote healing, wellness, coping and personal change, to be at the heart of the UNC Hospitals Bereavement Support Services. Specifically, these included poetry, writing, art, meditation, breathwork, and music. I integrated nature, using bamboo sticks and seashells for writing prompts, intentionally bringing the natural world inside the hospital whenever possible.

Celtic spirituality places equal emphasis on nature and Scripture. The crux is returning to your deeper, true self-your essence. The further away you get from that, it says, the more anxiety and fear you feel.

This reconciled my being a Christian minister and imposter syndrome. When I was young, my family attended a Unitarian Church in Massachusetts, but that faded away when we moved south to Charlotte. I was different from most of the other divinity school students and hadn't grown up in the church. Most of the time, I felt like a fraud among my southern friends and professional colleagues.

When my daughter Addie tells her friends I'm a minister, she adds, "She's not that kind of minister."

But I'd had this direct experience of the divine, and just couldn't shake it. Plus, I didn't want to. So, I kept it a secret. I would've gone to John Phillip Newell's church if I lived near him.

Of course, church wasn't where I felt connected to God. For many years, on Sundays I got out onto the tennis court to feel the sunshine and run around and laugh. Forgive me, but church services were, well, kind of boring. I preferred contemplative prayers with candles, lovely readings or psalms, and silence. And then I met John Philip Newell and experienced Celtic spirituality.

This dynamic spirituality is enamored with the soul and encourages you to listen deeply to it and what it knows. It's alive and full of wonder, and while Scripture was still challenging for me, this tradition looked at the Bible in a way I could get my head around. It is softer, more poetic. For instance, it often uses the word *beloved* for people and for God.

In a lovely passage from Newell's *Sacred Earth, Sacred Soul*, he writes, "In Celtic legend, the memory of John the Beloved, who, in leaning against Jesus at the Last Supper, was said to have heard the heartbeat of God. He became an image of the practice of listening for the beat of the sacred, deep in ourselves and one another, and deep in the body of the earth."

You get the point.

There are no doctrines or set of beliefs to adhere to in the Celtic way. It is also not bound by religion, but rather draws from the deep spiritual wisdom of many great religious traditions, including Native American spirituality and the wisdom of indigenous peoples throughout the world.

Here is the last word from me on Celtic spirituality. Anyone can access this way of seeing the world because it's based on the soul, the core of our being, and what it knows instinctively. The earth is sacred as well as is every human being. The Celtic tradition invites you to look for light in one another and in everything that has being.

There is something deep and powerful inside of us, who believes in us and keeps inviting us to take the next step. We all have it. Are you feeling it, too?

## REFLECTION QUESTIONS

I invite you to use the following prompts for reflection, journaling, or conversation:

- Given that there is something within each of us that is ancient, primordial, wise, and fearless, what would it look like for you to live out of the depths of your "deepest energies?"
- How do you use your active, creative imagination to dream and take you places?

# 11

## WHERE FAIRIES DWELL

"Nature is large enough to absorb your grief."
~Matthew Fox

"Let the fern unfurl your grieving,
let the heron still your breathing...."
~Julie Fowlis, Karine Polwart,
*The Lost Words Blessing*

A chaplain resident, who is Muslim, told me he believes nature is the soul of God. This made perfect sense since I feel closest to the Holy when I'm in nature. Maybe you do, too. In the Quran, it says, "If you want to see me and feel my existence, then look at nature. Look at the things I have created."

Nature cultivates contentment, raising your vibration naturally through wonder and beauty and awe. In the Celtic world, there is a deep connection to the rhythms of the natural world, the rhythms of the seasons, and the sacredness of the earth.

One of my favorite natural places is the lake at the townhomes where I lived after my divorce from Matt, with my two children. In the early mornings, I'd slip out the front door, cross the street, and head towards my sanctuary. Although there's an ordinary lake there, secretly to me it was my own magical forest kingdom.

In Celtic spirituality, this is known as a "thin" place, where the veil that separates worlds is porous. I'd speed up the closer I got to the threshold, which was the brush I had to duck under to cross through to the portal that led to the other side.

"Ahhhh," I breathed, sighing with relief once I crossed over.

Time changed there, slowed down, when I crossed the little bridge over the stream. It was *kairotic* or "God" time, an intimate time when I centered for my busy day as a single mother and palliative-care chaplain.

A friend of mine who is a shaman introduced me to Saint Brigid, the beloved Celtic Goddess from the 14th century. Brigid symbolizes radical hospitality and is known to be at the thresholds of life: birth, death, crossovers. She inspires creativity and inspiration and represents the crescent new moon phase of beginnings. St. Brigid embodies sacred feminine strength and stirred in me a hunger for creative expression, as well as illuminating the interrelationship of all things.

Bream fish, wild geese and their goslings, turtles, and playful otters, fill the lake. I became acutely aware of sights — the "no fishing sign" hammered to the tree across from where the little fish swim, the black snake that got caught in the drain below the bridge, that massive turtle, who had to be at least 100 years old, and sunned himself by the water's edge, beneath the weeping-willow branches that bend and sweep in the breeze.

Your senses couldn't help but tingle with delight! The plants and animals co-existed so seamlessly that my busy and taxing world and responsibilities slipped away.

In the midst of all this beauty, I kept an eye out for a glimpse of her, the most stunning creature of all. The great blue heron would appear out of nowhere, skimming across the top of the lake — poised, regal, silent, and confident. I watched and took mental notes.

This solitary one taught me helpful lessons while single parenting. The thing about herons, however, is that while they're solitary by day, they're not alone at night. And neither was I. The heron returns to her tree nest and rests in colonies. Similarly, when I came home after a long day, Noah and Addie were there, too.

The heron is known for her patience. I'm not a patient person by nature, and she taught me the benefits of this virtue. How to sit quietly and calmly wait for the rigors of life to ease, to be patient about finding a loving mate with whom to share my life. And herons' courtships and mating are known to be leisurely and relaxed, unlike many other birds.

Many spiritual seekers experience God's language as silence. One morning during a sunrise walk to the lake, my first sighting was a massive turtle moving at a snail's pace. Then I spotted something out of the corner of my eye. I wasn't sure it was the heron at first but had a hunch it was when I heard rustling nearby. Her still stance and focus draw my attention to her. She was standing in the woods! A rare treat for sure.

Then she saw me out of her side eye and took off in flight, in her gallant way. With her wide wingspan extended, she rose and moved to an old pipe sticking up out of the water on the other side of the lake. She was near the bridge I'd crossed earlier.

There are certain things I know are God things. That lake and the heron who comforted and taught me about patience and timing, are two of them. I knew the moment I laid eyes on her that it was the right thing to do to get up early and walk to the lake.

Your mind tells you, "It's only a 15-minute walk, what good will that do? You'll be late for work. You're tired and don't feel like walking today."

But you need to make time for silence and reflection. *Get out to the lake and walk.* You trust it. *It doesn't matter if it's just for five minutes.*

As German theologian Karl Rahner puts it, "Grace is another word for talking about the presence or self-communication of God." Just as the divine sent baby feathers on Cape Cod after Dad died and mom fell into a deep depression, God sent other birds — the Canada geese honking overhead surrounding my divorce from Matt, and the barred owl who woke me throughout my days at divinity and chaplain school. This time the Holy One sent the blue heron to show, *you are not alone.*

Herons share parenting duties, and I would've welcomed the help. My children, Addie and Noah were in elementary and middle school, respectively. Noah was struggling with stomach aches and migraines and suffice it to say, getting him to school was challenging.

I'd wake up in the morning wheezing from Marie, our French cat with digestive issues that we adopted to go with our nervous golden retriever, Harry. I thought I'd outgrown my cat allergies and Noah begged me for one, so I caved and adopted her. Tossing in bed worrying about how I'd manage to pay rent that month, or afford countless trips to the vet, or say, clothes for the kids, Marie nuzzled my neck. All the while, I sucked on an albuterol inhaler to breathe.

Of course, my friend Debby, who is also allergic to cats, urged over the phone, "You gotta get rid of that cat."

"Honk, honk, honk,"… a gaggle of geese flew overhead in the dark, just as panic set in. *Now how do they know my financial situation?* Somehow relieved, I'd wake up the kids, race out the door to drive them to school while still in my pajamas, and then get it together for work.

The first day of middle school for my son, Noah, ended shortly after the car line. Well, technically he never got out of our green Windstar van, affectionately known as the green monster, after the Red Sox's left-field wall at Fenway Park.

He was hunkered down and curled into a ball in the way back – the third row of seats. There was no way he was coming out.

Driving to school, I was feeling good about the new year: a fresh start – new school – a smaller charter one, recommended by a friend. It seemed like a perfect fit for my shy, cautious son. But my hopes were dashed when we pulled forward in the drop-off lane and it was Noah's turn to get out.

"Good morning! Welcome to Kestrel Heights!" A smiling, bubbly Mom volunteer slid open the van door.

But Noah didn't make any effort to move. My heart beat almost out of my chest, and I bit my lower lip. "It's okay, Noah, it's going to be fun!"

"I'm not going," he stated calmly and in a matter-of-fact manner.

"What do you mean, of course you are," I giggled nervously.

"No." Noah stared at me.

We were waved over to a designated parking spot, one I imagined they secure for reticent kids and nervous parents. We were holding up the line. *Late for work again,* I squinched up my face.

The cheery Mom and I caught eyes. "Bless your heart."

"Somebody get Coach C!" she called out. "He's our tennis coach and great with kids," she winked at me sympathetically as I pulled away.

The van door was still open when Coach Hunter Creedle appeared. He was buff, a 6'3" blonde Adonis, known as

Coach C, who assured me he'd coax Noah out. He had a 100 percent success rate. But Noah inched further into the bowels of the van.

The coach sat down and spoke with him rationally, "It's normal to feel scared when starting a new school. The fear isn't real, it's just in your head."

Then he calmly called Noah, "buddy," and bribed him with candy. This man's frustration was rising, as beads of sweat formed on his brow. Finally, he tried to physically pull Noah out.

*Bad idea.* I closed my eyes. Noah wedged himself farther away, between the seats.

"Okay, he's not coming out," Coach C announced in a 90 percent tone of voice.

I knew he wouldn't. I flashed back to Mommy's Morning Out when I was informed that Noah wasn't doing well in the toddlers' playgroup.

"These types of things don't work for some preschoolers," the director said, placating me. I must've looked like I'd been sent to the principal's office. "Bless your heart. Maybe try again next year."

"We'll try again tomorrow," Coach C offered. Then he left us and headed back toward the dwindling line.

The ride home was quiet. Noah did eventually go to school, despite setbacks with migraines and stomach aches. Eventually he grew out of his fears and learned how to adapt.

His father, Matt, observed, "It takes Noah about four years to get comfortable at a school, and just when it's time to move on to a new one, he hits his stride."

Meanwhile, I wasn't making ends meet with my chaplaincy salary. We needed extra money every month. Though it was stressful, money seemed to show up and we never missed a meal. I started to trust that. *Patience,* I thought of the heron standing motionless in the water, watching, and waiting for the correct moment to make a move.

The heron helped here, too. Doing a little research, I learned that they wade through water, stir up mud and silt to find food. Sometimes you must stir up some dirt. The heron shows you to do the legwork to turn something up. Get out there and put in the basic effort to lay the groundwork for future success. They wait patiently for the correct moment to make a move, and then strike!

Channeling St. Brigid's feminine strength, coupled with this knowledge, spurred me into action. Using my creativity whenever I panicked about money, friends helped me brainstorm ways to make some cash. I created side hustles, and it was actually kind of fun trying to solve the issue.

I started offering grief writing classes in the evening, called "Writing for Your Life." I'd get home from the hospital, whip up some dinner for Noah and Addie, and run over to the neighborhood clubhouse, where I held these groups, to set up for my 7:00 writing class.

Honestly, I was scared to death before each class. At one point I was offering two six-week groups simultaneously in the evening after work.

It was exhausting and exhilarating. I loved how the groups welded together so many things that were important to me and had been a part of my own healing and spirituality: female friendships, creativity, and writing.

Most of the women who registered had been in one of my talking grief groups offered through the hospital. Writing about loss offered a different, deeper mode of expression and untapped new perspectives and feelings.

One woman wrote about feeling invisible after her husband died. "Walking around the Harris Teeter grocery store and no one noticing me, reminded me I had no purpose anymore. When my husband was alive, I had one — to buy food to make for our dinner. Now it's just me with no appetite."

Another woman shared about working through her divorce and finding new love. "Your writing courses were a big part of my healing, a healing that makes my new relationship possible. I'm full of gratitude for you!"

Offering a creative outlet for people to heal and grow was rewarding; I was serving others and making some money. The bonus was the bright and cheery red cardinals who started showing up. They darted in front of the green monster on the way to my side hustles.

According to *Birds: a spiritual field guide*, the Cherokee believe that the cardinal is the daughter of the sun. "Examine the areas of your life in which you are or should be a leader. The cardinal tells you that you can handle it, and to believe in yourself."

One group member shared, "The cardinal is a symbol of coming out of your shell, stepping into your own greatness." If you are looking for a new way to express yourself, call on the cardinal to help you open up and get your creativity flowing. Their red feathers link this bird with fire, the element of activity, vitality, and passion.

In the mornings, on my walk to my van from the front door, I was accosted by these bright red birds. A male in full breeding plumage would dart past me, aiming for a nearby branch, with his mate following close behind. All the while I'd be rehearsing a presentation in my head for later that day.

Grief and joy are two sides of the same coin, like twins. The amount of joy we can feel is directly proportional to the amount of pain we've experienced. Isn't that fascinating?

Officiating weddings on the weekends became another money source, and probably my favorite. When a social worker and a nurse at the hospital asked if I could "marry" them, as an ordained minister, I was all in. I love working with couples and this ritual afforded me the opportunity to leave the hospital years later. Coaching engaged couples and officiating their weddings was fun and energizing!

My favorite part of the ceremony is being with the couple at the altar amidst their intimate exchanges. There's a moment, almost like magic, when we drop below the planning, their guests, even their nerves, and their love story culminates into a sacred ball, like a ball of energy. My job is to pass it to them to take with them into their marriage.

But I was tired. My day and night jobs, and now many weekends, were taking a toll. Single parenting two kids took everything I had. Looking back on it, I don't know how I did it.

I should mention two techniques that helped. They both calm your nerves and center you when feeling frightened about putting yourself out there. The first I picked up from a keynote speaker at an Association of Death Education Conference. I no longer remember his name, but I'll never forget the method he uses to quickly center and bring himself into the present moment.

"Now, I'm here," he says to himself as he transitions into a new situation.

It's a great way to leave behind what's happened so far in your day *and* any upcoming thing, and land completely where you are, with what's right in front of you in the moment. Naturally, I thought of the heron — *focus, concentration, patience*. I found myself saying this mantra (and still do) to focus while driving in the car on the way to places — to work, back home, and on the way to watch my kids' sporting events, teach and lead groups, and attend school functions.

The second method is great when you feel anxious about something you're about to do. For example, for me that's officiating a wedding, giving a presentation, leading a class, or facilitating a group. I adopted it from my former business coach, Christine Kane, who used to be a folk singer–songwriter. She traveled extensively to play live gigs and before stepping out onto the stage, she glanced over her right shoulder and whispered, "You got me?"

I love this gesture (or maybe it's a prayer) and say it every time I'm about to process down the aisle to officiate a wedding. This serves two purposes: first, it reminds me I'm not alone. Secondly, it takes the pressure off by reminding me it's not so much my words but God speaking through me.

I immediately feel myself relax and imagine that what comes out of my mouth may be just what the couple and their guests need to hear. I have about 20 minutes to share that message with them. Feel free to borrow either or both techniques the next time you feel nervous about a situation you're entering, or as my friend Emily would say, in a sticky wicket.

The heron and cardinals kept me company through all of this and made me smile. As theologian Jurgen Moltmann reminds, "To discover 'traces of God' in nature does not indeed save us, but it does make us wise...."

Here's the thing about grace, about "traces of God" reaching out to us. At least for me, it's hard to remember, to hold onto the goodness. I need constant reminders.

And when I forget because I can't stop the demands of life, they gently and silently keep coming back — like the feathers after dad died, the heron, the cardinals, the geese. Currently, a pair of mourning doves keep me company outside my bedroom window. Before my eyes are open, they sing their morning tune, "Coo, coo ... coo, coo, coo."

Regardless of who you are, or mistakes you've made, each of us is on a sacred journey and encounter "thin" places. We all receive little reminders that can help us to be fearless in the face of challenge, whether we know it or not. Have you ever picked up seashells on the beach, or found a sand dollar, and felt like you'd won Willy Wonka's golden ticket?

And when you don't know what to do and feel afraid, God's given us an amazing tool — our breath. This lovely gift brings us back to center with just a single breath. When you don't know what to do, you can just breathe.

*Ruah* is the Hebrew word for God's Spirit. *Ruah* also means breath, air, and wind in Scripture, reminding each of us of the physicality of God's presence in the world, that we are not alone. When you know that, St. Julian's words may echo in your ears, "All shall be well, and all shall be well, and all manner of thing shall be well."

I wrote the following poem, *A Single Sage*, after a particularly full day. A sage is defined as a wise, judicious, or prudent person. Unbeknownst to most of us, we're all called to become sages. It's my path and yours.

### A Single Sage

It's not easy being a sage when you're a single mom.
I want to watch the warbler whistle atop the
evergreen,
and ponder how the heron waits
and sits so patiently.
Yet I have Gatorade and granola bars to get
for my daughter's tennis team,
and watch her play so earnestly
it's such a joy for me.
I want to write pages
about the mysteries of life and death,
to muse over suffering and strength I see,
but my son just texted and struggles to breathe,
I need to get him some relief.
Off to his school I go, but not until I contemplate
this letter I just received.
An older widow lost her love

bereft of him is she.
"Thank you for remembering him"
is what she wrote to me.
But there are bills to pay, and animals to feed,
tutors to hire, and dinner to make.
And I just want to remember my love and me
strolling silently thru the woods
gathering stones and watching for feathers....

## REFLECTION QUESTIONS

I invite you to use the following prompts for reflection, journaling, or conversation:

- Do you have a sacred or "thin" place in your home? In nature? In your imagination? What are the elements that make it sacred?

- Are there spirit animals with whom you resonate? What characteristics do you resonate with?

- When you look back on your life, where do you scratch your head in amazement? What helped you navigate that part of your life? Where did you experience "traces of God?"

- What are your little reminders that keep you moving forward through life's challenges?

- I invite you to write a poem for any of the reflection questions above. Use the question as a prompt and see where you go with it.

# 12

## HOME IS WHERE
## YOUR HEART IS

"Only connect."
~E.M. Forster

"Awareness is the greatest agent of change."
~Eckhart Tolle

There was a clear shift in me. Something started changing in 2011, the year after I met with the psychic, Tomiko. She said it would for all of us, that we were entering the Age of Aquarius, a time of letting go of old ways and harnessing creative new ones. Little did anyone know the COVD pandemic was looming around the corner and would dramatically affect everyone on the planet.

"Our energy is shifting," Tomiko smiled, "our consciousness is opening to a higher vibration collectively."

While reading E.M. Forster's *Howard's End*, I was struck by the epigraph "Only connect." Someone once said to me that when it comes to having to do some*thing* or engage with some*one*, always choose human interaction. I started applying this to my exchanges. *How can I best connect with this person? Only connect* became my mantra.

I spent that Labor Day Weekend with Debby in Boston. We had a good visit, drinking coffee in the slow mornings and lots of wine in the evenings, catching up on our lives, laughing, and gossiping about people we'd been in school with. I read and slept in my goddaughter's bedroom, relaxing while Noah and Addie vacationed with their father. I was on a much-needed break from parental responsibilities.

While there, Debby and I drove to Gloucester to visit with her parents, Joe and Louise. Debby's Jewish family became mine as teenagers, and I often joined them in their home for Friday night Shabbat, the restful dinner focusing on family and spiritual oneness after a busy week.

I devoured pieces of challah bread and kreplach, small dumplings filled with potatoes and ground meat. My favorite hors d'oeuvres, these traditional potstickers are, interestingly, a food symbolizing the nature of Divine judgment.

"Shabbat shalom!" Debby's relatives greeted each other with good wishes as they gathered to eat dinner together, the start of their sabbath.

Secretly, I wished I was Jewish.

On this trip, Debby and I spent the night at her parents' home on the rocky shoreline that overlooked the Atlantic Ocean. My "Jewish mother," and one of my early saints, Louise, treated me as one of her own. For instance, that evening over cocktails, she pulled me aside, "I want you to know that you always have a home here. You have a place to stay if you ever need one." I'm not sure why, but those words meant more to me than just about any I'd ever heard.

Debby's parents landed in Gloucester because Joe spent fun-filled summers there while growing up with his many cousins. His mother, Sally, was one of seven sisters, and they lived in a huge white house on a hill, with a wraparound porch.

When he was older, Joe hoped to put down roots of his own in the beach town that brought him so much joy as a boy. Here is the brief story of how he made that happen.

But first I have to tell you that there are two ways of remembering your loved one. One is to look back and recollect past events and happy (or unhappy) times spent together. The other is to bring your loved one into the present and imagine them sitting with you. The latter is especially helpful if you have a decision to make and they were your person. The one you'd go to for advice.

So, Joe and Louise were looking around for a house to buy when they came upon *the* one. Joe had strong feelings about the peach-colored house with the wrap-around front porch on the water. He knew in his heart that he and his family — Louise, their two daughters, husbands, and five grandchildren — would be happy in this home for many years. But the house was too expensive and out of their price range.

We were standing in the front entryway looking out at the crashing waves while Joe spoke. "When my mother died, she left me some money, which is how we were able to buy a house. But the sellers wanted more than we could afford for this one."

As he was pondering his dilemma in the same spot where we were talking, Joe suddenly saw his mother out in the ocean, bobbing in the waves. She said to him, "Joe, it's all right. Buy this house. You can do it."

So, Joe and Louise bought their dream house and never looked back.

Here's the thing: I'm not sure if Joe summoned his mother to the present, or if she popped in, like Samantha's mother, Endora, on my favorite childhood television show, *Bewitched*. Either way, you get the picture.

Home was being redefined on this trip. We find home wherever we find it, and it may not be the home of our family of origin. I left Debby and Boston contemplating what home means, and flew to Santa Fe, New Mexico where I'd signed up for a three-day retreat, *Contemplative Practice and Rituals in Service to the Dying*, way up in the hills at the Upaya Zen Center. Founder, Buddhist teacher, and end-of-life pioneer, Joan Halifax, co-led the retreat with Frank Ostaseki, founder of the Zen Hospice in San Francisco.

I'd heard Joan speak a few months earlier at a chaplains' conference and was mesmerized by her talk "Being with Dying: Cultivating a Fearless and Compassionate Heart."

"I work with the dying because it is deep," she said.

Nodding, I understood. *Yes.*

At the retreat, social workers, chaplains, physicians, and other health-care workers gathered to learn about deep self-care and ways to stay grounded and self-regulate, while working with dying people and their families. This aligned well with my "only connect" theme, and the trip set the course for the rest of my career as a palliative-care chaplain.

Upon arrival, we were assigned a room and roommate. We slept on futon mattresses on the floor. We ate delicious vegetarian food prepared by Jane Fonda's personal chef. As a carnivore, I never would've known there was no meat in any of dishes if we hadn't been told. These sumptuous meals were some of the best I've ever eaten in my life. We all took turns on kitchen duty and simultaneously agreed.

You learned right away that meditation is a way of befriending who you already are, and that regular meditation trains the practitioner to be less bothered by external stimuli. All it takes is establishing a regular practice. Another important benefit of meditation is that you begin to feel at home everywhere. This was especially helpful given my recent revelations about home.

By the way, meditation also happens to be a cheap and easy way to strengthen your immune system. We meditated first thing in the morning, after each teaching session, before and after lunch, before dinner, and the last thing of the day.

Joan began the meditations with, "What time is it? Now. Where are we? Here."

This brings us to the matter of the present moment. The fastest way for you to get to the present moment is through your breath. There are two great gifts of being in the present moment, the now.

The first is power. There's so much potential in this moment, right now. You get to choose how you want to respond to what's happening right in front of you. The second is rest. When you're fully in this moment, you rest your weary noggin from fretting about the past and worrying about the future, essentially from being lost in thought.

Meditation teaches you there is an observer in your mind, a witness who watches your thoughts coming up, and this creates a sense of separation. You are not your thoughts. Training to quiet your mind through consistent, daily practice, provides a space to notice what is below the surface and is coming up.

Sitting with what is, and not pushing it away, teaches you to be less reactive. You notice a space, a separation between the thoughts coming up. You observe them, but are not them, because someone (you), the conscious part of you, is aware of them.

This can be hard to wrap your head around at first. Becoming consciously aware of your thoughts is step number one. For example, years ago I flew to Boston to see family, and my brother David, who was living there at the time, picked me up from Logan Airport. "How's it going?" he asked.

"Good," I answered, "except every time I think of something good about my life, a bad thought comes in and sabotages it."

"That's not good," he responded.

At the time, I thought that was my lot, just the way I was and that there was nothing I could do about it. Now I know better. You can replace negative thoughts with positive, life-giving, better ones.

As Joan points out, "Suffering begets suffering. Don't do that!"

She and Frank taught us how to cultivate pro-social and virtuous behaviors by repeating systematic mettas, or loving-kindness meditations. Just like Tiffany! I recognized these prayers as the ones she was sending after her lung transplant from her hospital bed.

The mettas create the capacity to be open and kind to all beings, including yourself. The wholesome qualities of gratefulness, equanimity, compassion, joy, and kindness are cultivated.

"These qualities create a tiller to put your hand on in rough seas," Joan explained. The sailboat image is a helpful way of remembering to stay balanced.

Carrying heavy, or "lower vibrational thoughts" around with me since childhood, I was eager to replace them with lighter, higher vibrational ones. As Albert Einstein teaches us, "The most important decision we make is whether we believe we live in a friendly or hostile universe." I was beginning to trust that the "other shoe" didn't have to drop and was being given new tools to ensure that didn't happen.

The mettas are offered to five categories of beings: yourself, your friends, neutral beings (or patients), difficult people, and all beings. We sat and repeated them silently to each category:

*May I be free & safe from all danger.*
*May you be free & safe from all danger,*
*May all beings be free & safe from all danger....*

And then you do the same with the next metta, and so on...

> *May I be happy and peaceful.*
> *May I be healthy and strong.*
> *May I be free of physical suffering....*

Repeating these positive statements and sending them out into the Universe replaced old, unhealthy and unhelpful thoughts, with pro-social, healthier ones. You think you want happiness, but what you really want is relief from your looping negative thoughts.

We were encouraged to make the mettas our own and add to them:

> *May I meet my soulmate and love of my life.*
> *May I be filled with joy.*
> *May I overflow with abundance.*
> *May I be grateful for my life....*

While at Upaya, it happened to be the 10th anniversary of the September 11th attacks, which made flying and traveling an interesting and nerve-racking time. If you're old enough, that's one of those events, like the Challenger exploding on national television, where you know where you were when it happened.

I was teaching pre-school in Addie's classroom. We'd just finished free dancing to *"This Little Light of Mine"* and were getting ready for snack time with goldfish, cheese cubes, and lemonade. One of the teachers from another classroom, who also happened to be my neighbor, came running in and whispered in my ear that a plane flew into the twin towers. Of course, the rest is unfortunate history.

I flew home from Upaya on 9/11/2011 and it was a big deal in the airports. American flags hung on all spare wall space and security was tightened. The airports felt tense, and everyone seemed a little more nervous than usual about flying that day.

Riding in the shuttle on the way to the Santa Fe Airport, the retreatants started talking about dating. One of the passengers from Tennessee told us about a dating site she was on called DharmaMatch.com. "It's a free, spiritual kind of Match.com."

I was skeptical. I hadn't had much luck on dating sites and recently averted a disaster with a stalker. I made a pledge to go off all on-line dating sites.

My sister-in-law, Nina, applauded my decision. "Taking a break sounds like a good idea."

I comforted myself, *you can't get everything you want in life, right?* I had a meaningful career and two great kids. I would focus on those things — the good that I had. Love wasn't in the cards for me this go around. Nonetheless, I jotted down DharmaMatch.com on my conference booklet and made a mental note to check it out.

When I got home, I made a list of about ten or more of my own mettas or positive statements on an index card. I studied my list and memorized them as best I could. I've always been good at memorization and give a nod to Wordly Wise, my seventh-grade comprehensive vocabulary program, which helped me learn the meaning and utilization of "big" words. Thank God, since standardized tests were my nemesis. Believe me.

Although I felt good about knowing my mettas by heart, I still slipped the index card into my back pocket just in case. Then took them with me when my golden retriever, Harry, and I went for our daily 3.5 trail walk.

Over and over, whispering to myself. "*May I be peaceful. May I be happy. May I be safe. May I overflow with abundance – health wealth, joy, and happiness. May I meet the man of my dreams.*" Climbing the steepest hill on the trail I'd gasp, "*May I be grateful for this day.*"

Then I started actively visualizing my soul mate.

Debby told me a year or so earlier, "This time you need someone who's emotionally available, grounded, easy on the eyes, and oh, who has a job."

I took it to heart and started dreaming up my tall, ruggedly handsome, soulful man. I'd light a candle before meditating, a simple ritual that fires up your imagination.

DharmaMatch.com was different from other dating sites because you share your favorite books. Mine were, Nan Merrill's *Psalms for Praying, The Sacred Journey,* by Frederick Buechner, *Gifts from the Sea,* by Anne Morrow-Lindberg, *The Secret World of Hildegard, The Velveteen Rabbit,* and *Bird by Bird,* by Anne Lamott.

I kept up with my affirmations but forgot about DharmaMatch.com. I'd only been on it a couple times, and honestly it attracted some kooky people. But Addie noticed an unread message once while playing a game on my laptop, so we took a peek.

The message simply said, "Would love to find out more about you."

While this mystery man's profile looked intriguing, he didn't post a picture. Addie said there must be something wrong with him.

She helped me compose my response, "Hi, thanks for your message. Nice profile. Do you have a photo?"

The picture we got back would change the course of my life, yet again. There he was – my man. Tall and ruggedly handsome, with his blue blazar and khakis, Tim was standing with his hands in his pockets and a sheepish, sweet smile.

"He's cute!" Addie declared with surprise.

"Yeah," I sighed, smiling with relief.

I tell Tim now that I manifested him. I dreamt him up and brought him to me. He came from my creative imagination and the mettas that I held steadfast to and believed with all my heart.

After 28 messages on DharmaMatch.com, we met for dinner for our first date. It was as if we'd known each other all our lives.

We both marvel now that we never met until that time. Three of our five books on DharmaMatch were the same and had the contemplative thread in common. He was into the desert fathers, and meditation, and was the university chaplain at a prestigious college. How had our paths never crossed? Perhaps we weren't ready.

It didn't take us long to find out we had lived across the street from each other in Charlotte, 25 years earlier. He was the pastor of a Methodist Church, living in the parsonage. I was a party-girl debutante, working for my father and trying to figure out what I wanted to do when I grew up.

We both frequented Berrybrook Farms Natural Foods, a health-food store down the street from our nearby homes, but somehow never ran into each other. Tim's five years older than me and I'm pretty sure we wouldn't have connected then, but who knows? It comforts me knowing he was nearby all those years.

Our orbits were circling each other, but it wasn't time for us to meet then. Repeating positive, affirmative statements helped me find Tim, the love of my life, and my "grown-up" relationship.

And suddenly the air was full of dancing dragonflies, delightfully darting in front of me, presenting themselves, as if showing off. A quick Google search told me that two together serve as a confirmation that you're in a mature relationship that is one of a kind. These magical, shining dragonflies landed on my car antennae, and flirted with me on one my favorite walks at a wildlife preserve and bird sanctuary near the hospital.

According to dragonflytransitions.com, a wilderness education website, "In almost every part of the world, the dragonfly symbolizes change, transformation, adaptability, and self-realization. The change that is often referred to has its source in mental and emotional maturity and understanding the deeper meaning of life."

One more thing … after our first few dates, Tim gave me a gift: a silver necklace with a dragonfly pendant. When I got home, this giddily spilled out:

### Crazy in Love

Crazy in love
Crazy in love
That's how I feel about you.
I've not known you for long,
yet haven't I known you forever?
You are an archetype, *my* archetype-
kind, wise, mindful, caring, curious, strong,
creative, open, funny, sensitive, and charming
to name a few
of the attributes
that drew me to you.
You are the perfect mate for me, my beloved.
I feel so much joy and bliss when I am near you
I can barely contain it. Name it. Understand it.
Is this what love is? It must be. I haven't known
before now.
How can it be that I've been given this grace,
this chance, this good fortune?
Haven't I been given enough?
All I want to do is look up and out and beyond

*and within* and shout gratitude for this gift of you!
Thank you for bringing him to me!
For knowing, he is the one whose side I want to be by.
Yet, words do not describe
how grateful I feel for you being in my life.
So I pray my vibration
will overflow with appreciation
for the abundance of crazy love
I feel for you.

## REFLECTION QUESTIONS

I invite you to use the following prompts for reflection, journaling, or conversation:

- Write your own mettas. What's most important to include? (Bonus – write it on an index card or maybe in the notes section of your cell phone to keep with you.)
- What are the stories you tell about who you are that might need to change?
- What is the bigger story of who you are?
- What new story is emerging?
- Have you ever been "adopted" by another family? If so, what was that like for you?
- What images come up when you think of home?

# 13

## WHAT MATTERS?

"Let death be what takes us,
not lack of imagination."
~B.J. Miller

"My soul, when I tend to it, is a far more expansive
and fascinating source of my guidance than my
ego will ever be, because my soul desires one thing:
wonder. And since creativity is my most efficient
pathway to wonder,
I take refuge there, and it feeds my soul,
(and it quiets the hungry ghost)."
~Elizabeth Gilbert, *Big Magic*

U pon returning to work at the hospital after my trip to New Mexico, I started applying my contemplative practices and rituals with patients, their families, students, and staff. I offered short meditations to help ground staff and experimented with providing reflective writing sessions for caregivers with my writer friend, Carol. As author Mirabai Starr notes, "Expressive writing is the most powerful portal to transformation that I know of."

Poetic metaphors are a great language tool because they explain the unknown in terms of the known. For example, Denise Levertov's descriptive *Talking to Grief* uses the image of a stray dog as a metaphor for grief. Here's an excerpt:

> Ah, grief, I should not treat you
> like a homeless dog
> who comes to the back door
> for a crust, for a meatless bone.
> I should trust you ... give you
> your own corner,
> a worn mat to lie on,
> your own water dish.

Another helpful writing tool is writing a dialogue with an aspect of yourself you may be struggling with or curious about. It reads like a screenplay.

I had a talk with my creativity (C):

Me: What is it that you want?

C: A voice. I just want to be heard, like all the time.

Me: But why? Why are you so eager to be heard?

C: Because you are a creative person at your core. Someone who thrives on creativity. And serving others. And serving others through your creativity. It's the basis of who you are.

Me: Sometimes it's hard to keep up with your demands. I'm tired and want to rest.

C: Ahhh, but it's also where you come most fully alive. Yes, it's tiring ... and enlivening. You are right at the edge of existence, and it pushes you.

Me: Yes, that makes sense. Will I get used to the pushing? The nerves?

C: I don't know. But you will meet God there every time.

Accompanying one of my colleagues to her daily radiation treatments for breast cancer is where the seeds germinated for the hospital writing program. Each weekday, after heading to the basement for her "medicine," I'd sit in the waiting room with strangers, the same familiar faces, sitting idly, anxiously marking time. We'd wave or nod to each other in recognition and return to mindlessly reading a magazine or book.

*What if they had a space to connect and process together?* Such a need.

Perhaps you've been there, for yourself or with a loved one. Repeatedly returning to the cold, dark, bowels of a hospital, for a regimen where electromagnetic waves, or radiation beams, target a specific area of the body and try to alter the DNA makeup of a cancerous tumor, causing it to shrink or die.

The idea wouldn't leave: *it would be so helpful for this group, the same people who gather in this little room every day, to connect in a meaningful way, sharing what was going on beneath the surface.*

My writer friend, Carol, and I often talked about collaborating and offering a writing program at the hospital for people, a thoughtful way of processing what was happening for them. Years earlier, Carol's six-week-old infant son, Malcolm, died on the operating table from complications during heart surgery. His pediatric cardiothoracic surgeon was trying to correct his serious heart murmur. After weeks of tubes, EKGs, and operations, a heart-shattered Carol and her husband left the "peds" waiting room and hospital, for the last time, empty-handed.

"Don't go see him," the well-groomed social worker advised. "There's the door ... just leave," she said emphatically. And so, not knowing that cradling their tiny son one more time would provide a balm for them, they did just that.

Carol's harrowing grief led her to write a memoir, *Losing Malcolm: A Mother's Journey Through Grief,* and to develop programs to help other bereaved mothers connect through the act of writing. Her life's work became educating and supporting others through writing and sharing about their losses.

So, Carol and I decided to give it a go, and our vision materialized with a writing group in the cancer hospital, *Writing for Caregivers*. At the first session we had two women show up, wives of men going through cancer treatment.

Writing to the simple prompt, *What matters?* Elaine wrote, "I feel so helpless. I can't believe this is happening to Brad. I don't know what to do. What matters is getting him the best care possible and being by his side."

Amazed at how brave people were in writing and sharing, I wanted to train to co-facilitate these reflective writing groups and hold this sacred space with Carol. This led me to her mentor, Pat Schneider, founder of Amherst Writers & Artists (AWA). Pat believed everyone is a writer and if not on paper, then in the air, in our minds.

We expanded our group to include patients, people in the community, and even staff, and renamed our program *Writing for Resilience.* Imagine writing with a mixture of patients, caregivers, and health-care professionals and then bravely sharing what you wrote (if you wanted to). This levels the playing field since everyone is courageously bearing witness to each other.

Abby, a medical student with a penchant for writing, attended the group as often as her hectic schedule allowed. One time she wrote about her cadaver from her Surgery 203 Anatomy class, a rite of passage in which students in their first year of medical training dissect a human cadaver.

Iris is the name Abby gave her donor. "A blank stare greeted me, but I was looking, searching, for something more. I pictured how her pacemaker used to pump blood, switching past the valves, letting her be. I think efforts of emotional dissociation can only cover up reality for so long.

We're piecing together who she was, how she functioned, and how her physical body allowed her to live.

"Even as I held her heart, I was reminded of the person. Glancing at her fingernails and toenails, I saw they were painted with a faded, red hue, which offered hopeful reassurance. Whoever Iris really was it wouldn't be far off to assume she was a fashionista."

Abby gave me permission to share her piece when I spoke at the annual Anatomy Memorial Service, a time set aside to thank the donors and their loved ones for their invaluable contributions to UNC Medical School and their students.

Carol and I co-led the confidential, weekly writing group, *Writing for Resilience,* in the hospital for eight years. Every Tuesday at noon, for an hour, we held space in the chapel for people to take time to remember, to get thoughts down, to reflect through writing, and to share with others.

We intentionally moved our chairs into a circle to write together. Some spiritual traditions believe a circle represents the Divine life-force or Spirit that keeps our reality in motion. It is symbolic of vitality, wholeness, completion, and perfection.

A group that writes together and shares is a powerful combination. Magic happens. As one regular participant wrote, "People come here when something is going on in their life ~ a cancer diagnosis, treatment, a separation, a divorce, a death, an empty nest, and then sometimes they leave for a time and then come back."

We modeled our writing group after Pat's AWA method and used various prompts — quotes, objects, poems or single words, and other ways to tap into creative expression. The idea is to come at something 'slant,' or from the side, not head on, which may make it easier to approach. These prompts help you to begin to gently explore feelings that silence or limit you, so that you may move more freely forward.

Here's how Writing for Resilience worked: we offered a prompt, we all wrote for a bit, and then had an opportunity to share, for those who felt so inclined. Sharing wasn't required, although there's a theory that sharing doubles the healing. You can sometimes hear your story and the solution you've been looking for in another's, and theirs in yours. Something powerful happens when speaking your words out loud.

Author Flannery O'Connor said it best, "The life you save may very well be your own."

However, we encouraged people to try not to write with sharing in mind. "Write for yourself," Carol encouraged. "Let your mind take you where it will — perhaps to private unexplored places or maybe to an incident from this morning, or your past, a fresh idea, or a worn-out one. Just go with whatever comes to you. So often we are surprised and informed by where our writing takes us — if we let it."

If someone started apologizing for their shitty writing, or clarifying details, one of us would interject, "This is all first-draft stuff. Don't feel you need to explain. You read only what's on your page. Just read the words. This keeps the group safe — it gives some structure, a container, and provides boundaries. It's a writing group, not a talking group."

One day, Gail showed up, sat down, and started writing. She was a regular outpatient at the hospital and walked in pulling an oxygen tank behind her obese frame. She had a thin tube under her nose that administered extra oxygen as needed. Gail bravely shared that she'd passed by the chapel door many times while we were meeting but was too nervous to come in and join us.

What pushed her to enter, she said, is a quote by the Nigerian author Chinua Achebe, "When suffering knocks at your door and you say there is no seat for him, he tells you not to worry because he has brought his own stool."

Gail wrote beautiful pieces about trees and how she communicated with them after her parents died. When her younger sister suffered multiple injuries in a tragic car accident, Gail was left to care for her. She wrote about her struggles with her own health while caring for a family member.

Gail lived in an apartment beneath a successful businesswoman, and put into words how in the morning, she'd hear her getting ready for work. "Her heels click-clack across the hardwood floors above. I imagine when she's putting on her lipstick and drinking her coffee, reading the newspaper and then flipping off the lights, before leaving her apartment, rushing for her car to get to an important meeting."

Being on disability, Gail longed to have a fulfilling career. As she shared this piece, a single tear rolled down her cheek and dropped onto her oxygen line. After a while Gail stopped coming to write with us.

When I ran into her at the hospital Starbucks a few months later, I barely recognized her. Gail was 50 pounds lighter, had no oxygen tank behind her, and shared that she'd started facilitating a weekly writing group at the Catholic student center!

Carol and I periodically started sessions with our original question, *what matters?* Believe me, you can answer differently every time. You might start out with superficial concerns, but if you stay with it, you'll find you're off and running in new, often deeper directions.

That's one of the beauties of a writing group. You start out in one place and end up in another. Say you're writing about your broken heart. Well, you may end up laughing and running on the beach with a former lover from when you were 20 years old, reminding you that you weren't always sad and lonely. There's a sliver of hope there leading you to believe you may actually laugh and have sex again.

The group helped me heal as well. I wrote about my father's illness and death, my mother's subsequent health issues, patients I worked with, my childhood, my two divorces, and falling in love with Tim. Knowing I had a place to dump my thoughts and feelings each week was a relief. Seeds of this book emerged, as well.

In one piece, I asked God what I should write about in a book, and the immediate response I got back, "Tell them who I (God) am!"

Hearing how people navigated challenging times was inspiring and taught me how to write, too, by listening to how others crafted their first-draft pieces. One cancer patient, Melissa, wrote about her losses from breast cancer and her journey of who she was becoming. She wrote herself into a new identity. "There is a process to being able to trust and hope again and believe good things can happen."

After two years of writing on and off with our group, cancer-free Melissa accepted a job in Denver, Colorado to start a new career as a physical therapist at a medical clinic there.

Through the writing, I often came up with ideas for my work as the palliative care team's chaplain. For instance, while responding to Mary Oliver's poem *When I Am Among Trees*, one line stayed with me:

"When I am among the trees, especially the willows and the honey locust, equally the beech, the oaks and the pines, they give off such hints of gladness. I would almost say that they save me, and daily."

*What would 'save' these professional health-care providers who carry around a lot of cumulative grief with them daily?* They bond quickly and deeply with their patients who have serious illnesses, and their loss can feel personal when their patients die or are discharged, often to Hospice.

Processing passive and marginalized or disenfranchised grief is important so that it doesn't fester and become stuck. Since reflection is an antidote to burnout, writing about painful experiences would be one way to proactively bring them to the surface and often shift them. This led to a monthly reflective writing session for the palliative-care team.

Let me just say a little about palliative care here because it's so often misunderstood and confusing for people. The goal of palliative care is to improve quality of life for both the patient and their family, using an interdisciplinary team approach. It's appropriate at any stage of a chronic illness.

Palliative care in the hospital setting provides specialized medical care for people living with serious illness. These heroic health professionals focus on symptom-relief management and the stress of living with a life-threatening illness, helping with medical decision making and offering support to both patient and family.

Whenever possible, the palliative-care team discharged a patient from the hospital to Hospice, either at home or in a facility. Hospice works with patients and their families at the end of their lives. Often, people think that palliative care and Hospice are the same thing. While they often work together and complement each other, they are separate entities.

Most mornings as the team's chaplain, I'd lead a grounding meditation before the physician on-call for the week started "running the list" of all the seriously ill patients on the service and their family needs and complications. These compassionate caregivers give daily updates on visits and brainstorm ways to make their patients' and families' quality of life better, always with the highest regard. "We plan for the worst and hope for the best," was the objective I heard more than once shared with families from our dedicated physicians.

Remembering the power of mettas, my meditations usually included a brief breathing exercise and setting an intention for the day. "What do you most want to happen today, and how do you want to feel?"

We'd close with a poem, and honestly, poet Mary Oliver was their favorite. The team dubbed her palliative care's patron saint of poetry. Someone once told me that poetry is the language of the soul, and Mary's universal poems speak directly to your soul. She puts words to spirit in nature and illustrates how we're all sacred beings with a full range of emotions. Mary also gives language to gratitude, and while she didn't proclaim a certain faith, she was deeply spiritual.

Spending time with people who are dying, you notice that *what matters* boils down to similar themes. For example, as layers of ego are stripped away by the disease process, the essence of a person remains. The team eagerly reflected on such themes during our monthly writing sessions.

While the palliative care fellow physicians were required to attend as part of their year-long curriculum, many of the other interdisciplinary team members joined us to write as well. One fellow, Katie, shared her reflections to *what matters?*

> "As I have moved further along in my training, I have realized that there are actually fewer things that 'matter' truly in our lives, but those that do matter are much more similar between people than we all realize.
>
> "Often the things that we focus on every single day, worry about and stress about become less important. What becomes crucial in the crises of our lives are our connections with others and the impact our lives have made on those we care about. We all seek to feel loved and also feel our love for those we most care about. We hope that in some way we will build a legacy that continues to guide or improve people's lives after we have gone.
>
> "Some days I will find that I have driven home from work without realizing what I am doing — my mind is so pre-occupied with all the little things to do that night, the next day or the next

week. Then I come home and see my two-year-old
son and refocus on my love and connection to him
and everything else seems less important."

### *Praying, by Mary Oliver*

It doesn't have to be
the blue iris, it could be
weeds in a vacant lot, or a few
small stones; just
pay attention, then patch
a few words together and don't try
to make them elaborate, this isn't
a contest but the doorway
into thanks, and a silence in which
another voice may speak.

## REFLECTION QUESTIONS

I invite you to use the following prompts for reflection,
journaling, or conversation:

- Are there conversations you're having with yourself
  that are recurring? How might these be a reflection
  of a part of yourself that might be in pain?
- What thoughts, feelings, emotions, bodily sensations,
  or memories do you naturally turn away from?
- What matters? Write a stream of consciousness about
  what comes up for you. Don't edit it, just see what
  comes. Start with a list if that's helpful.
- What do you want most to happen today, and how
  do you want to feel?
- If you feel so inclined, consider checking out a writing
  group in your area to join.

# 14

## THE GOSPEL OF GRATEFULNESS

"Surprise is the seed of gratefulness. Become aware of
surprises. Relish surprise as life's gift."
~Brother David Stendl-Rast

"Gratitude for the gift of life is the primary
wellspring of all religions, the hallmark of the mystic,
the source of all true art."
~Joanna Macy

"When before the beauty of a sunset
or a mountain, you pause and exclaim,
'Ah,' you are participating in Divinity."
~Ancient Hindu text

"Listen carefully... and incline the ear of your heart."
~Rule of St. Benedict

Debby attended a Paul McCartney Concert at Fenway
Park, part of the 2022 Got Back tour. At 80 years
old, Sir Paul played a full three-and a-half hour set
without even a pee break. The thing that struck Debby the
most however, besides his amazing music, was his humility.

"He sang a song written by each of the Beatles and dedicated it to them," she beamed. "Sir Paul profusely thanked his band members, his crew, the crowd, the lighting guys. British, American, and Ukrainian Flags were flying side by side."

Paul McCartney closed his show with his song *The End*,

"And in the end
the love you take
is equal to the love you make."

"What a great role model for all of us! The guy has more money than God and he's so humble and grateful," Debby recounted, shaking her head.

Expressing gratitude is a spiritual practice, a strand of spirituality that you can cultivate. It doesn't contain dogma or religious beliefs, although every religion emphasizes gratefulness — it's at the heart of Christianity, Judaism, Islam, Buddhism, and Hinduism.

Gratefulness is a radical, proactive approach to life in all its fullness, rather than a momentary reaction to having your needs met. It reverses your priorities, turns them on their head, and helps you appreciate the people and things you already have, instead of longing for what you don't have.

Research reveals that we live at least half of our lives — 50 to *70* percent in compulsive thinking, busyness, and distractions. We aren't present to what's in front of us. We spend most of our time worrying about the future and what's going to happen, or we're stuck in the past, regretting or ashamed about things long gone.

We look for distractions because the present is too painful. Worrying is using your imagination to create something you don't want. Research shows that 90 percent of what we worry about doesn't happen!

With gratefulness, you don't have to change your life, you just change how you approach life. For example, many terminally ill patients in the hospital long to go outdoors. They want to look up at the sky and the clouds, feel the sun, or rain, smell a flower. We walk outside every day and mostly take these opportunities for granted. My yoga teacher friend, Angela, said to me once, "Anything we take for granted is lost to our experience. Anything we do mindfully can bring joy."

Kristi Nelson, Executive Director of Gratefulness.org, says, "Gratefulness beckons us toward greater contentment, joy, agency in every moment of our lives. By cultivating gratefulness as a foundational way of experiencing life, we can access a deeper, more reliable reservoir of happiness."

You know people who have everything in the world and yet they aren't happy. And you know people who have experienced devastating loss who are happy. They are happy because they are grateful.

Nelson admonishes, "It is NOT happiness that makes us grateful. It is gratefulness that makes us happy."

Brother David Steindl-Rast, Benedictine monk, author, and scholar, developed practical theories about grateful living. An international spokesperson for interfaith dialogue, at 80 years old, Brother David founded the Network for Grateful Living, an interactive website that promotes the practice. You decide for yourself, but I say Brother David is a saint.

He says, "We live in a Universe that talks to us, and once we recognize that, it's quite natural to listen because we want to hear what the message is."

What?! How amazing is this? This affirmed what I was experiencing with birds, synchronicities, coincidences, and my glimpses of Spirit and cosmic intelligence. I was listening.

I read some years ago that Oprah starts each morning, "Thank you for this day, the best day of my life." I adopted this habit and started saying it upon waking. It was another way of replacing the adage from my childhood of "waiting (anxiously) for the other shoe to drop." Grateful living says the shoe doesn't drop! You can expect something good to happen. Such a game-changer!

Gratefulness actually happens before thinking. Those breathtaking moments of awe and wonderment while watching the sun set or a full moon in the sky have the power to move you in ways you never thought possible. In those tender seconds before your thoughts take over, an inexplicable energy surges through you – elevating your frequency towards a higher level of consciousness that's capable of healing you, as well as positively impacting others.

You can use your thinking to tap into the creative intelligence that animates life and guides you towards transformation. When you surrender yourself willingly, this transformative power flows through you - awakening surprise and cultivating a deep sense of gratitude for the gift of life. This sparks an unstoppable force within which expands into generosity as your sight is opened up to those who are suffering. And like meditation, gratefulness naturally promotes the prosocial behaviors of joy, wonder, forgiveness, and compassion that feed your soul.

As Trappist monk and writer Thomas Merton reflected, "To be grateful is to recognize the love of God in everything … every breath we draw is a gift … every moment of existence is a grace."

Now, you don't have to be grateful for everything that happens — your loved one dies, or a mass shooting occurs, but you are given an opportunity to respond in love. Perhaps you develop deeper compassion and can respond out of that. You become responsible for what happens *through* you not *to* you. Ask yourself, *what would my life be like if I lived more from a place of gratitude?*

Gratefulness is another way of being present, paying attention. It engages mindfulness and holds the key that allows you to access the same physical, emotional, psychological, and spiritual benefits of those times when you are filled with gratitude about something. In those times, our brains release dopamine and serotonin, the two crucial neurotransmitters responsible for our emotions, and they make us feel "good." They enhance our mood immediately, making us feel happy from the inside.

Environmental activist Joanna Macy says, "In times of turmoil and danger, gratitude helps to steady and ground us. It brings us into presence, and our full presence is perhaps the best offering we can make to our world."

Neuroplasticity, also known as brain plasticity, is the ability of the brain to change continuously throughout your life. Research shows that many aspects of the brain can be altered to generate new neurons and connect them with the rest of the brain, even through adulthood. For example, the practice of long-term meditation can influence the physical structure in the brain. No matter what your age is, your brain can rewire — it has that ability!

University of North Carolina psychology Professor Barbara Frederickson says, "The negative screams, but the positive only whispers." This is so true. For instance, you know how when you complete a project and your friend or boss or partner remarks on how well you did? Then they mention one tiny piece that could've been better? I don't know about you, but I hear that little criticism more loudly than all the compliments combined.

We all have a pronounced negativity bias. It comes from the oldest, lower part of our brains, known as the reptilian brain, that has allowed us to survive as a species. You may have heard it called or referred to as the lizard brain, the animal brain, or the ancient brain. All these names reference the fact that this is the most primitive part of your brain.

The lower brain is the earliest brain. It is the part of your brain that is concerned with the most basic of functions, and those functions have to do with survival. So, the lower brain is tasked with ensuring survival, and looking out for danger or negativity.

As it turns out though, every time there's a moment full of awe or wonder, there's an opportunity for you to create a new pathway. So many of us need to cultivate new pathways because our present pathways become roadways, which become interstate highways. And by the time we're adults we often are on automatic pilot with our thoughts. The same hardwired thoughts travel our well-worn superhighways in our brains. Here's the good news: you can train your brain to do something new and different.

In the Buddhist tradition, there's an exercise taught to young children. It's called the ten-finger gratitude exercise. Children are taught to count ten things they are grateful for each day, one thing for each finger. After only two weeks of practicing this, your brain creates a new neural pathway.

Our brains like homework, the science says, so if you commit to naming ten things you notice today that went well, that you appreciate and give thanks for, the universe will bend over backward to line up ten more for you the next day, and so on. It's like a muscle — the more you use it, the stronger it gets.

Plus, there's scientific research that suggests that gratitude diffuses difficult emotions, and health benefits can result. One researcher in this field is Robert Emmons, a psychology professor at the University of California at Davis. What Emmons found is that those who kept a gratitude journal experienced significant psychological, physical, and social benefits; in fact, he found a 25 percent improvement in overall health and well-being in comparison with groups focusing on what had gone wrong each day.

At this point, you're probably not shocked to learn this research prompted me to buy gratitude journals for the Bereavement Support Service. I started teaching about the benefits of a gratitude practice and handing out tiny journals to staff, groups I led, as well as to some families and patients. For people in the hospital and their personal and professional caregivers, gratitude offers a helpful mindset shift.

Theodore Roosevelt once said, "Comparison is the thief of joy." Practicing gratitude is an antidote to comparing yourself and your life to others. It turns the focus back onto you and what you have to be thankful for. Everyone has something, whether it's your breath, having something to eat, or eyes to see with.

Having a gratitude practice was especially helpful to me as a divorced person. Sometimes I found myself jealously looking at married couples and daydreaming of how nice it must be to have someone to bounce stuff off of, help with the kids, or take walks with. Receiving holiday cards from friends and seeing their beautiful, happy families was especially difficult.

Brother David says the most important aspect of living gratefully, is *trusting life,* especially when we feel anxious of fearful. Whatever your life situation, every human being every day must make a practical choice between trusting life or not trusting life. Again and again in life, you may be tempted to distrust and feel fearful. When I get triggered by an old tape looping in my head, I naturally go there. Consciously becoming aware of the anxiety or fear, feeling it, and letting it naturally pass, like all emotions do, helps. It takes some of the urgency away.

Brother David says, "If you try out distrusting life and always questioning life, you find that it makes you miserable... you can try trusting life and whatever comes up, saying, "Well, maybe I don't like it, but I trust that life gives me good things — that life is trustworthy." Living that way, with a spirit of gratitude, opens you up to all kinds of possibilities. Every moment can be an invitation to ask yourself, "What's the opportunity here?" By recognizing and seizing these opportunities, you have the chance for transformation and growth.

In *Bird by Bird*, writer Anne Lamott uses eating broccoli as a metaphor for trusting life. She borrowed it from an old Mel Brooks routine in "The 2000 Year Old Man." A psychiatrist tells his patient, "Listen to your broccoli and your broccoli will tell you how to eat it." This is an important lesson for life. It means that when you don't know what to do, you become still, and life will tell you what to do. Listen quietly to what life is trying to tell you.

My tennis-pro friend Emily says it this way. "You only have to hit the next ball back. Just hit the ball that's coming toward you."

So, your purpose of life is really to live, and not be on automatic pilot. Stop every now and then to respond to the organic flow of life. You may need to train yourself to do this, but you *can* do it. It's impossible for your brain to be grateful and anxious at the same time.

It turns out, even gratitude appreciates being noticed. Every living organism has a consciousness and appreciates and responds to being noticed, being seen. Did you know that if you appreciate a flower, it will open up a little more and grow faster? It's the same idea. Gratitude feeds on itself.

Since I learned this, I've been talking to my plants. "Good morning, lovelies," I say as I spritz them with water. I swear they respond by growing a little taller that day.

Whatever you notice and give thanks for thrives.

Buddhist teacher Joan Halifax tells us, "It's not the cards you were dealt, it's how you play them."

What you pay attention to expands. The great news here is that you can water the seeds you want to grow by paying attention to them. You can start new seed streams. Living gratefully is an attitude toward life and you can respond to whatever shows up with curiosity and appreciation.

And closing reflective writing groups with a gratitude list is the best way I know of sending people out into the world.

## REFLECTION QUESTIONS

I invite you to use the following prompts for reflection, journaling, or conversation:

- Consider starting a gratitude journal. Write a list of 10 things you're grateful for today. Commit to this practice for two weeks and see what happens.
- What would your life be like if you lived more from a place of gratitude?

# 15

## MOTHER'S LITTLE HELPER

"You have power over your mind — not outside
events. Realize this, and you will find strength."
~Marcus Aurelius

"I want to love a person freely, including all her
secrets. I want to love in this person someone she
doesn't know. I want to meet her between the words,
beneath language."
~ Helene Cixous

"Daring to dream what is deepest in our
collective longings is what makes us most
human and fully alive."
~Wendy Wright

"Your most secret wound is the doorway…"
~Ivan Granger

"Most importantly, remain being Heidi. Don't change. We love you as you are, Hydra!" This is how my father closed the letter he wrote to me when he was dying. Let me just say, my father had nicknames for everyone and everything on the planet.

I was Hydra, short for Hydra-Headed thing. Now, if you Google this, what you find is not the most endearing image you presume a father would nickname his eldest daughter. For instance, Encyclopedia Britannica says, in Greek legend, circa 1599, the Hydra-Headed Thing is "a gigantic water-snake like monster with nine heads, one of which was immortal." I'm glad I didn't look this up as a child. Merriam-Webster says the adjective hydra-headed means "having many centers or branches." I like that better. I'm going with that.

His other prominent nicknames in my family were my mother Barbara who was Rab, short for Rabrab (Barbara backwards, mostly). Her station wagons over the years were always "the sandbox" since she never cleaned them out and pails of sand covered the floorboards from summer outings at the Cape.

David, my older brother, who played sports and came home covered in mud and left his clothes piled up in his bedroom, was Dirty Dave; my younger brother was Scooter, and my sister was "the Littlest." Now there's a couple reasons for hers; she was the youngest child, and tiny when she was born.

Dad meant well and loved me, yet this is what I mean. I *wanted* to shift my thinking, not to become someone else, but rather more truly and authentically myself. I wanted to align my personality with something other than my family of origin. Ironically, Dad's illness and death is what revived me and pointed me toward doing just that.

Like so many of us, I grew up in a dysfunctional environment. My father ran his German grandfather's textile business and often seemed tense and distracted. He had a competitive and volatile personality, and drank to relieve his stress. My parents had late-night parties with lots of booze and smoking and noise. They often argued at night in their bedroom.

My room was the closest to theirs upstairs in our house and I was awakened by their fights. Kneeling next to my bed after my "Now I lay me down to sleep" prayers, I begged God to make my parents stop drinking and hating each other so much, and for our family to be "normal." I cried myself to sleep while my mother and father yelled at each other so loudly, our whole house shook.

I believed if I prayed hard enough, God would "fix" things for the better. In addition, if I was perfect enough my parents would be happier.

Despite my family's private struggles, outwardly we showed a different face. We were an "all-American family", with young, good-looking, and athletic parents and four children in the right order: boy, girl, boy, girl. I led a privileged life of private schools, country clubs, and summers on Cape Cod. Although I had "everything in the world" as my mother often reminded me, I felt empty inside, as if something was missing.

In the morning after the drunken battles, I'd asked my mother at the breakfast table, "Is everything all right with you and Dad? I heard you fighting last night."

She'd respond brightly each time, "Yes, we're fine. We weren't fighting. Everything's fine."

*What? You were fighting —— I thought you were gonna kill each other!* But I nodded even though I knew she was lying because it was important to stay on her good side. There was no one else to take care of us. I needed a place to sleep, and someone to buy food to eat.

One morning I walked into my parent's bedroom, still dark with the curtains drawn, and saw by my mother's side of the bed, their framed wedding portrait, face down on the carpet smashed, shattered glass everywhere.

I'd heard her crying in the bathroom the night before and asked innocently, "Why were you crying last night?"

"I wasn't crying, it was my allergies." My mother doesn't have allergies.

Listening to parents fighting is not a safe and secure feeling. I felt frightened listening to them go at each other. Part of me clung to my mother's lies, wanting desperately to believe they were true. If so, we must be safe. My mother repeatedly denied their fights, so after a while I acquiesced and stopped asking. I got into the habit of doubting the voice that was telling me quite clearly what was really going on. I figured; I must be wrong. But I was right.

My childhood was chaotic. It was unpredictable. Life was one way at night and another during the day. It was confusing and I carried a lot of heavy thoughts with me throughout the day. I was a worried child on the inside, while my outer self appeared placid.

As early as elementary school, I tried sharing with a classmate during recess, "Do your parents fight at night?"

She responded with a silent, blank stare.

Embarrassed and ashamed for revealing this family secret, I kept my stress to myself. I absorbed and internalized my parents' angst and carried it securely locked away inside of me for years. Shame loves to stay hidden, and I lugged that shame around like a suitcase for a long time.

Shame is "I am bad," not "I feel badly." It's an intrinsic, destructive feeling. I had a voice; I just didn't use it. I chose not to express myself. It was safer to stay quiet than risk upsetting my parents.

Instead, I played roles to appease them. Like many girls, as the eldest daughter of four siblings, I was taught at a young age to put my mother's needs first. I feared not adhering to this unspoken rule because she was so unhappy. I learned this lesson well and felt the responsibility of being the eldest girl. It weighed heavily, yet I took it on myself to help with my younger siblings, appointing myself as their caretaker.

I made it my mission to ease my parents' tension. I'd make my father laugh by doing impersonations when he got home from work. I played "mother's little helper" to try and keep Mom happy, cleaning the kitchen and tidying the house when she was out, to surprise her when she got home.

Sublimating my wishes to keep the peace came with perks. On several occasions when stressed, my mother threatened my siblings that she was going on a vacation to Bermuda, leaving them at home and only taking me with her. We never actually took that trip, but I was ready to pack a bag at a moment's notice.

In middle school, our class took the Johari Window quiz, a technique that aims to help people understand their emotional and physical relationship with self and other people. The window consists of four panes of human interaction: open, hidden, blind and unknown. My "hidden" window was three times bigger than the other three, revealing that I kept most of my thoughts and feelings to myself. Ashamed about this, I naturally covered my results and hid them from the rest of the class.

Shame thrives on staying hidden. If you shed light on shame, it dissipates. Sharing is like kryptonite to shame. But the key is, you've got to allow yourself to be vulnerable, to let the guard down that you've learned to keep up to protect yourself. University of Houston research Professor and author Brené Brown calls the shield "armoring up." We spend our whole lives creating a shield to protect ourselves, so that we're safely hidden and not hurt. Brown says, "Vulnerability is what I most want to see in you, and what I fear most you'll see in me."

While I was self-protecting, I was also blocking off connection. We have so many roles placed upon us – mother or father, daughter or son, sister or brother, wife or husband, lover, cook, chaplain. Fill in the blank. Here's the thing, though: when we play this role long enough, we have a hard time separating ourselves from the role. We believe that's who we are.

Joan Halifax says, "When our identity gets tied up with our deeds, our deeds become a drag."

The Celtic tradition believes we suffer from soul-forgetfulness. We've forgotten who we are, what we know — personally and collectively in the deepest part of ourselves — a collective knowing. Listening to your soul and treating it as sacred is a different way of seeing and moving forward. Using your imagination is one way of reawakening your soul. What makes your heart sing? What have you forgotten that you used to love doing?

Limiting belief systems are the number one obstacle to fulfilling life plans. How do they affect who you've become and what you've been able to do in your life? There's a difference between who you think you're supposed to be versus who you really are. Locking ourselves into some roles, we start believing we can't do anything else. Specifically, the very thing we want to do, were born to do.

I carried my "helper" role into my marriages, which transferred easily onto my husbands, continuing to keep the focus off me. Blocks are also roles we play, hiding from our original knowing of our soul's purpose.

Buried under layers of conditioning from our family of origin, religious traditions, and our culture, we slowly start to forget our larger, deeper purpose — our soul's work that is unique to us.

Yet how do you align with the deepest parts of yourself? Your willingness to alter your looping beliefs from the past. Until you work on patterns from your upbringing, it's hard to do that.

Learning to speak your truth involves risk, letting yourself be seen. Empathy is key, Brown says, which is the antidote to shame. Empathy is like getting down in the trenches, putting yourself in another's shoes, actively and curiously listening with an open mind. Finding a non-judgmental conversation partner who can help you sift through your life and excavate your treasure, the richest, most alive part of yourself, perhaps for the first time, is one way.

I was fortunate to have two caring souls help me reconnect with my center. Karen, my spiritual director, whom I met with monthly about where God was showing up in my life; and my therapist. I went back to therapy to work on the shame I carried with me. I was choosing emotionally unavailable men because I thought I didn't deserve a loving partner. I was ready to replace that old, distorted belief with a new, fresh one and make a positive change.

My therapist told me I was caught in a loop of repetitive compulsion. She told me I unconsciously chose unavailable men, because if I could help them become more open and able to connect emotionally, then there'd be hope for my mother. Of course, I never changed them. It was only after I became aware of the pattern that I was able to work on breaking it. Slowly, I did break the pattern and now have an authentic and loving relationship with Tim.

Presbyterian minister William Sloane Coffin observed, "We put our best foot forward, but it's the other one that needs the attention." We connect with people through the "other foot." I tested out being more vulnerable in other areas of my life.

For instance, I started saying, "I love you," to my mother when we hung up from phone conversations. I extended it to my siblings, then close friends. I don't remember my parents saying this when saying good-bye on the phone and it felt risky at first. But Mom started saying it back, as did others. Your presence, it turns out, is more important than your role.

Intrigued by Brene's research, I traveled to San Antonio, along with Tim, to train with her in her shame-resilience program. As a certified shame-resilience facilitator, I taught and mentored chaplain students and individuals on how to lower their protective "shields" and live more whole-heartedly.

Empowering people to excavate their gifts from their deepest wounds or grief became a passion. Women from the grief groups, once they were further along in their grief work, got curious as a new identity emerged, sometimes reclaiming parts of themselves they'd forgotten. I led vision board retreats where individuals who were hungry for a new life expressed their desires. Often their wildest dreams on their boards became a reality.

Paradoxically, a time of mourning or grief, or post-pandemic, is a ripe time to do this work. When off center and vulnerable, you're more open to change. You may hear things differently, let in something new, something you may have otherwise ignored. This is a great starting place — when you're malleable and somewhat raw.

This led to leading retreats on creativity. One of my mentors for these is Christian mystic Hildegard von Bingen. She became a writer, scientist, composer, and abbess of a convent, but not at first.

It turns out hiding brilliance is not new. Hildegard, born in Germany in the Middle Ages, had visions but lived in an age when women had no power, so she kept her gifts a secret. She feared sharing them, but hiding her gifts gave her debilitating headaches.

Hildegard heard God speak to her from within, "You must stop hiding your light. You must let other people see what you see. You must let the light inside of you shine out."

Reluctantly, Hildegard started sharing her visions. Her headaches disappeared. She wrote music, scientific books on plants and medicine, and eventually was elevated to sainthood by the Catholic Church.

Hildegard exemplifies bravely reviving and sharing our "visions." For Hildegard von Bingen, all creativity was one and the same, and it all came from the same source, God. This "feather on the breath of God," as she referred to herself, models women breaking barriers.

We each have a part to play in this universe, we are part of the whole. You develop your gifts, and I develop mine, to further human evolution. For you have what I need, and I have what you need. We need each other.

There's a deeper part of you waiting to be rediscovered and experienced, beyond what society says. This takes courage because like my father, your loved ones and friends may want you the way you are. But you need to let the butterfly out of the jar. Do you have a dream that's yet to be fulfilled? Who is the butterfly of you?

One of Oprah's favorite books is Michael Singer's *The Untethered Soul*. He writes, "You must be willing to let go of your personal, psychological self (your identity and complaining voice). In order to be who you are, you must be able to let go of who you think you are ... you meditate to find the center to be able to let go."

Meditation and introspection lead to an awakened state of consciousness that allows us to transcend ego and habitual thought patterns. This brings a sense of freedom to realize that you are not your thoughts. Rather, you're connected to a larger whole, to a Divine intelligence, beyond the human mind. That's why sometimes in meditation you have a feeling of unity, or togetherness.

Connecting with this intelligence, this intuition, opens a new reality. This is how you become the creator of your own life, your own experience, and you discover that you have a wealth of knowledge and wisdom inside you. The more you shine your own light, the more others will be inspired and attracted to you.

So, part of this life's purpose is self-healing, liberating yourself. What is your gift? What gives you the most joy? Expressing yourself from the heart, doing what feels natural and fulfilling at a personal level, always aligns with your aim to contribute something good and powerful to this world.

What do you want your ripple effect to be when you're gone? What would happen, if just for today, you stop repeating the same old stories to yourself. Change the script and you change your world. Past events are past and past stories are told. Find a conversation partner to help you and go write a new life for yourself. Within every person there's a seed of wisdom. Define your wisdom. Develop your gifts to serve the world, the greater good. What will happen through you?

I'll wrap up this chapter on roles, with a poem by William Martin:

> Crack yourself open!
> What use is it to continue to hide
> behind your facades and roles?
> Why waste your energy playing games?
> Isn't it time to cry your tears,
> to shout your passion,
> to dance like Zorba,
> and to let your soul touch
> the Soul of the world?

## REFLECTION QUESTIONS

I invite you to use the following prompts for reflection, journaling, or conversation:

- Did you have a nickname as a child? If so, what was it?
- What significant events in your life have shifted your thinking or changed your trajectory?

- What roles have you locked yourself into?
- What is your soul's work? Is there a part of you that you're hiding?
- Where are you finding alignment with the deepest part of yourself?
- Do you have a part to play in the universe? What might it be?
- What old scripts need to be discarded?
- Are there aspects of your life you feel shame around? How does it manifest? How does it prevent you from living into your authentic self?
- Do you still have treasures that remain buried? What are those treasures?
- Looking back on your life, what are you most proud of?

# 16
## FREEDOM

"Listen to your life. See it for the fathomless mystery
it is. In the boredom and the pain of it no less than in
the excitement and gladness: touch, taste, smell your
way to the holy and hidden heart of it because in the
last analysis all moments are key moments,
and life itself is grace."
~Frederick Buechner

"May the long time sun shine upon you,
all love surround you, and the pure light within you,
guide your way on."
~Snautum Kaur

"May you be well in body, mind, and soul. And may
you be strong in the work of healing the world."
~Celtic Blessing

"We are here, but not forever."
~ Natalie Goldberg

My direct experience of God woke me up with a personal invitation into relationship, communicating that we are not alone and left to our own devices to figure everything out in this life. This grace I received restored a sense of well-being deep within me and set me on, what the Celtic world calls a peregrination, a pilgrimage, some radically fresh way not known before. Grief taught me that we live in a creative world with divine intelligence. And working with individuals at the end of their lives reminded me that this life is not a dress rehearsal.

We're not promised a certain amount of time here on this earth. I'm not and you're not. In fact, life is really short. It's fleeting, and we mistakenly think we have discretionary time to figure things out and do all the things we want to do. But the only moment we have to do this work, is now, the present moment.

Let me share a story with you: my brother-in-law Ed died from pancreatic cancer shortly after he turned 59 years old. He was athletic and strong, an avid runner, an Outward-Bound Instructor, and did ski patrol work for a resort in Colorado at different times in his life. He went for walks daily with his wife, Robin, almost to the end of his life.

Toward the very end however, Ed suffered and withdrew, pushing Robin and their teenage daughter away. Many of his final days and nights were spent in a hospital bed tucked away upstairs in their home, with his eyes shut, taking only sips of water. He didn't want to be touched, although his wife longed to wrap her arms around him. Robin was shattered, worried this is how Ed would die.

But Ed rallied. He stepped up at the very end of his life for his family. He turned a corner and vocalized what was happening to him. It was as if he was in control one last time and being coached on what he needed to do. Ed had unfinished business before he left this world.

Joan Halifax says, "When you spend time with a dying person, you discover that the human spirit has the power to come forth in the middle of crisis and suffering in ways we can't imagine. Over and over, I have seen ordinary people — afraid, angry, confused — awakened into profound wisdom and understanding. If you want to find out how to live, spend some time with a dying person."

Ed reconnected. His daughter climbed into bed with him, gently rubbing his head, threading her arm through his with his fingers wrapped around her wrist. He let his family get close and love him. Ed was surrounded by a lot of love. Robin told him it was okay to let go, that she and their daughter would be all right.

But Ed asked Robin to call his brother, my husband, Tim, and she held up the phone as he spoke.

"Hey man," Ed whispered. He barely said anything else, and later, Robin shared with Tim that Ed listened intently to what Tim was saying to him.

Ed and Tim's father, who died earlier that year, was visiting Ed regularly, as he vacillated between this world and the next.

For example, on her final visit, Patricia, their sister, said to Ed, "Now you may think I'm crazy, but I sense someone in the room with us."

"I know, it's Dad. He's sitting right there," Ed stated matter-of-factly, pointing to the empty chair to the right of his sister.

At Christmastime, a few months before he died, Ed shared with Tim, "I wish I knew when I was younger what I know now. I would've focused on very different things."

In Celtic spirituality, Saint Brigid is known to be at the threshold of death, showing people how to cross over. There is a moment soon before earthly life ends, when a person drops below the fear, below the pain, when perhaps loved ones come from across the veil with the guidance of Saint Brigid to escort them.

When a family who were acquaintances of ours from summers on Cape Cod lost their mother, her daughter reached out me on Facebook. She messaged me to share the surprising last words her mother ever spoke, which included my father. "Oh my God, it's David Gessner!"

I don't remember my father being terribly fond of this woman, but he was a hospitable guy. Maybe he was there helping Mrs. Statesman cross over. Who's to say?

There's a moment when a person is dying, when it becomes all right to drop their earthly body, to set it free, and allow it to become divine, yet still staying connected to everyone and everything. Perhaps we become part of the thin, invisible, gossamer thread we follow.

Maybe Ed's father was there helping him.

At the very end, after connecting with each of his family members, with his eyes closed, Ed murmured to Robin, "You can't believe how beautiful this is."

And before his last breath, Ed whispered peacefully, "I'm coming."

Neurosurgeon Eben Alexander, who had a near-death experience, says in his book *Living in a Mindful Universe*, "The reuniting with the infinitely loving creative force at the death of the body is a most beautiful lesson of the true oneness underlying our existence, the eternity of spirit and interconnectedness of all souls."

The key thing to remember is that existence doesn't end with the death of the physical body. Our connection doesn't end there. As poet W.H. Auden writes, "Death ends a life, not a relationship." Our continued intentional interaction with our loved one is part of the process, as we seem to be forever connected through our love for them.

Not everyone experiences this phenomenon, but many families of people who've died share stories of how their loved ones reach out to them as if to let them know they are okay, through synchronicities, dreams, and nature. Hospice and palliative care health-care workers who have frequent experience with the dying know this deep truth because they have seen examples of it time and time again.

Let me tell you about Michael, a physician who joined our grief group after his wife, Anna, unexpectedly died after a short illness. He beautifully describes sensing Anna's presence. I never found out why she was planning the water blessing ceremony he mentions, but Anna loved the sacredness of nature, including water, and went to the woods often to be restored and to seek answers to her questions.

"It was Wednesday evening after Anna's memorial," Michael explained. "My oldest daughter and sister had left that morning. The house was quiet as I sat down in the solarium looking out on the woods where Anna spent her last weeks. I decided to turn on the CD player and as I sat down, I began to hear sounds of water dripping coming from the speakers and then water over stones, like the small rivers we listened to in the Big Horn mountains when camping.

"Anna was planning a water blessing ceremony for a women's center where she volunteered before she became ill. She had always followed the phases of the moon and knew the phase on any given day, symbolic of the feminine for her. As I sat down and began to marvel at the sounds of water, I looked up and in a small window near the ceiling of the solarium was a full moon. The synchronicity of the moon rising to that point at that time with the water sounds created in me a sense of wonder and awe. Despite my science-driven bully of my rational mind, I felt a sense of connection with Anna."

Death is a great teacher. One of the secondary benefits of working with terminally ill patients and their families is that you learn to stop taking things for granted. You don't have unlimited time here on earth to fulfill your hopes and dreams. You remember to live each moment fully because when you die, you'll no longer be able to fill the roles you were busy playing.

Part of the chaplain's job is helping an individual sift through memories and experiences, the good and bad, to find some peace before dying. Ed seemed to turn the corner after spending some time with a Buddhist hospice chaplain.

Rather than waiting for that life review at the end, what if you enacted a daily or weekly review, where notable events are assessed as potential lessons? Such reviews can bring significant life lessons to the surface while you still have time to make changes to your attitudes and behaviors.

When my childhood summer friend, Sarah, died of lymphoma, I traveled back to Cape Cod for her memorial. We were supposed to get together the previous summer while I was vacationing there but canceled our visit because too much was going on with my family. I told myself I'd catch her next time, assuming we had a lifetime ahead. I didn't know she was sick.

Sarah was three years older than I and the big sister I always wished for. I idolized her. She was pretty, smart, witty, and very kind. When we were growing up, she wasn't like the other older girls who snubbed my friends and me for being younger.

Sarah and I played tennis together every summer. She had a wicked forehand, very Chrissy Evert-like with her free hand gracefully placed out in front of her to meet the ball. We played on the Dennis Yacht Club tennis team. Don't be fooled by the "yacht" part — our club met in an oversized shingled shack, but we were proud of it, nonetheless.

The summer I was 11 years old, and Sarah was 14, our team did better than usual, and we were invited to play in a tournament on Martha's Vineyard. Ingrid, our Swedish tennis pro, was our chaperone and accompanied us over on the ferry.

I don't remember playing any tennis or how we fared, but my guess is not very well. I also don't remember caring much, as my attention was on Sarah and how lucky I was to be hanging out with her, away from home, and all the older girls who stole her away from me.

One evening on the island, our team walked down the middle of the cobblestone streets after dinner looking for an ice-cream shop. I was riding on top of Sarah's shoulders and as we strolled by the harbor, we noticed a massive shark hanging on a hook.

"Is it real?" we wondered.

As we got closer, we could see the colossal fish was fake. An onlooker informed us there was a movie being filmed called *Jaws*. It was the mechanical shark used in the movie!

While back on the Cape for Sarah's memorial, I walked down to the "Little Beach" where I'd been a thousand times before, many of those with Sarah. I could see up on the bluff the cottage her family rented every August.

The sun was setting, and it took me back to a time years before when I was in this exact spot, alone at sunset. It was low tide, and the mussel shells and seaweed were painting the hard, wet sand. Gulls flocked near the jetty, their melancholy cry "mewing" as they fished for their dinner.

It is said the gull's call can sound like laughter or something sad. Gulls symbolize freedom, balance, and adaptability, and remind us that everything has a flip side. My mother wrote a little book about a seagull when I was young.

"Hi, I'm Seymour, a seagull by the sea," she read to me, "and as a rule I'm as busy as a buzzing bee...."

But in this memory, I was on Jasper, an Appalachian horse that belonged to our wayward neighbor. Earlier that summer I'd heard her whinnying from my upstairs bedroom window. Jumping out of bed, I ventured through the woods following her neighs and grunts.

Toby was a "towney," what the Cape Cod locals were called. He was a lobsterman who lived with his wife, Judy, two daughters, Hannah and Chelsey, and nephew, Derek. His yard was strewn with lobster traps, wooden buoys, and nets.

Derek took care of the four horses that lived in the make-shift barn and stalls behind their garage. I'd wander over and feed Jasper carrots and watch Derek groom the horses.

I became an unofficial babysitter for Toby's girls that summer as their mother was often nowhere to be seen. Turns out, Toby had a violent temper and Judy was often recovering from her previous night's beatings inside the house before her night shifts as a waitress.

I started to ride Jasper around their yard, getting the feel of her. One evening, Derek suggested I take Jasper out for a walk around the neck, our cluster of cottages surrounded by the the bay and harbor. Excited, I intuitively found myself heading for the "little" beach, the nickname we gave the sandy patch of shoreline closest to our cottage, complete with jetties jutting out into the bay.

As we trotted onto the dunes, the sun was hitting the western skyline toward Boston and pink spread out like a brilliant blanket over the water. The full moon was rising to the east, connecting with the depths of the ocean, getting ready to shine in the night sky.

The tide was low, making the small beach much larger than when the tide is high, and the wet, hard sand sprinkled with starfish, mussels, and minnows. The flat surface was perfect for Jasper's steady footing. There was an intimacy in having this liminal space to myself, where shore and salty sea meet. Unusual for this time of year when tourists and resi-dents alike normally came here to witness the kaleidoscope of colors in the sky.

But the beach was mine this evening, and I gave Jasper a squeeze with my heels. Her trot became a canter, and bareback, it felt good to feel the primordial wind against my face, my hair flowing behind me. Wanting to go faster, we broke into a gallop leaving behind any lingering fear.

The last of the sun's rays were shining down, as if just for me, and I felt free and joyful, what spiritual teacher and author Eckhardt Tolle calls "vibrantly alive peace." It was if Jasper and I were dancing in the breeze amidst the sea salt, sand, and sun's brilliance, the moon patiently waiting to rise.

Hungarian psychologist Mihaly Csikszentmihalyi, who coined the term 'flow' describes the feeling by saying, "The ego falls away. Time flies. Every action, movement, and thought follows inevitably from the previous one, like playing jazz. Your whole being is involved, and you're using your skills to the utmost."

In that moment, anything could happen. I was completely free of worries, fully present, happy, and flowing with life.

Seagulls mewing their "freedom" above me, Mary Oliver's words echoed from within:

You do not have to be good.
You do not have to walk on your knees
For a hundred miles through the desert, repenting.
You only have to let the soft animal of your body
love what it loves.

I know I can return to those precious moments whenever I want to feel that joy and freedom. You, too, can use your active imagination to bring an important time to you in the present.

"You are the living light in every respect. From you all light shines," Saint Hildegard said. "Your unique brilliance, full of colors, has a radiance that is inimitably yours, wealth of experiences, learnings that brought you to this point, make up your unique journey. Spread your inner light and life of light. Go out and shine in the world."

What would happen if each one of us concentrated on discovering and bringing forth the light from within? How might our relationships and our world change — for ourselves, with each other, and with God? Your work is to bring forth that Light from the depths and beam it out into our troubled world.

For you have what I need. And I have what you need. We need each other. In the mystical Gospel of John, Christ says, "That they all may be one." (John 17:21) This is taught in the Hindu and Jewish traditions, as well as by the great Sufi mystic poets. It is taught in all the great religions of all time. We are all one with the universal consciousness, the Universal Oneness of God.

Surgeon and author Atul Gawande writes in *Being Mortal*, "How is dying ever acceptable at all? The only way it is, is because we as human beings live for something bigger than ourselves." After his father's death, he traveled to India with his sister and mother, to spread his father's ashes on the Ganges River, upon his request.

Gawande says, "Literally millions of families have brought the ashes of somebody in their family who's died to the Ganges. That connection to people going back that many years makes you feel like you're connected to that many years going forward, as well."

When my own father died, we returned his ashes to his beloved Cape Cod Bay. Our family went out on his boat the *Sea-Ges* on a calm evening at sunset and told stories of how he loved to be out there on the ocean spending time with his friends and families. My mother will join him there most likely sooner than later.

Life is sacred. It's incredibly brief and tomorrow is not promised to any of us. You will never be able to accomplish everything you want to accomplish. And your history does not determine your present, or your future.

Life is asking something of you, not next week, or next year, but right now, just as you are. Nothing you have done or not done can prevent you from answering. And life is waiting for your response.

As we come to the end of our journey together, I invite you to close your eyes, and bring your awareness to your breathing. Just notice the breath coming in, and the breath going out.

And when you are ready, and only when you are ready, ask yourself the question poet Mary Oliver poses in her poem *The Summer Day*, paraphrased here: What is it I plan to do with my one wild and precious life?

A leaf is falling
smiling at the clouds
in total freedom
and trust
The divine nature
holds all in its embrace
In the heart of a bustling city
In the soul of a forest
A glowing ray shines through
A lonely seagull glides over the ocean
While the desert sings its soulful song
A whisper
a cry
a child is born
and someone sheds tears of joy
while
somewhere else
someone else
cries tears of sadness
The world goes on turning
The divine nature is present in all things.
~ Toni Carmine Salerno

## REFLECTION QUESTIONS

I invite you to use the following prompts for reflection, journaling, or conversation:

- What is it that you want to get done in your life with the time you have left?
- What changes do you need to make for that happen?
- What obstacles have you overcome?
- People who impact us live on. Who lives on for you?
- How do *you* want to be remembered?
- What legacy have you already left behind?
- If you could instill one virtue or value in the next generation, what would it be? Why?
- What have been the happiest of times?
- What path is emerging for you now?